Fatal Choice

Fatal Choice

by

John Q. Baucom

MOODY PRESS

CHICAGO

Moody Press, a ministry of the Moody Bible Institute, is designed for education, evangelization, and edification. If we may assist you in knowing more about Christ and the Chirstian life, please write us without obligation: Moody Press, c/o MLM, Chicago, Illinois 60610

Library of Congress Cataloging-in-Publication Data

Baucom, John Q.
  Fatal choice.

  1. Youth—United States—Suicidal behavior.
  2. Adolescent psychology—United States.   3. Suicide—
United States—Prevention.   I. Title.
HV6546.B38   1986   362.2   85-29648
ISBN 0-8024-2533-X

  1 2 3 4 5 Printing/RR/Year 90 89 88 87 86

Printed in the United States of America

To some of the best therapists I know:

Ross Campbell, M.D.
George Karasievch, Psy.D.
Mickey Nies, Ph.D.

Thanks for everything.

PUBLISHER'S PREFACE

This book is an analysis of the teenage suicide phenomenon that is spreading like an epidemic among our young people. This material is not intended to be a theological treatise on suicide or its related issues. Rather, it is the author's desire to offer the reader the benefit of his training, experience, and professional judgment in an effort to provide help for parents, teachers, pastors, and other counselors in saving our teenagers from the tragedy of suicide. Dr. Baucom presents a needed study of the signs and signals that alert us to those young people with suicidal tendencies and suggests answers that are consistent with the principles of the Word of God and sound professional practice.

ACKNOWLEDGMENTS

I wish to express my deepest gratitude to several people for their assistance in the preparation of this manuscript. Scott Keegan and Chuck Wagner were instrumental in getting the process started. Dr. Winford Hendrix has been a patient listener, friend, and adviser. Bennie Keplinger spent hours in reading and editing. Dr. Paul Suttles, Dr. Dave Killen, and Dr. Murdock Smith assisted and gave input at important times. Dana Gould has provided inspiration, encouragement, and has been a great "coach." And I give special kudos to Debbie, who literally stole hours away from nowhere to type and retype. I thank each of you.

CONTENTS

FOREWORD

Our country is at war.

This warfare is not only for the lives of our teenagers; it is also for their minds and spirits. Authorities indicate that up to 6,000 adolescents will take their own lives in the next twelve months. That fact is startling. Equally shocking is the 2 million who will attempt suicide in that same time period. Clearly, society needs a collective reaction not only to call attention to the crisis but to mobilize a response.

There is another trend that is also troubling. It has been estimated that more than 80 percent of the teenagers being raised in the church are leaving and will probably never return. It could be that the origins for both the suicides mentioned above and the spiritual suicide I refer to can be found in the same source.

The answer is certainly not simple. It is exceptionally complex. It is also sometimes unnerving to focus on an issue this intimately. It is a troubling crisis. And to truly understand it is going to be equally troubling.

My friend and colleague John Baucom is one of the few people in the country who is qualified to write this book. He blends material from his personal life, academic training, and professional experience to weave an educational and enthralling discussion of this complex problem. He is also bold enough to imply there is room for change.

This is a book that demanded to be written. It now equally demands to be read. I encourage you to read it and then read it again. The material can be a catalyst for change in this time of national crisis.

D. ROSS CAMPBELL, M.D.

PREFACE

The idea for this book has its origins in modern American society and the social dilemmas we face. It is intended for anyone who is a parent, teacher, counselor, or friend of an adolescent. My goal as the author is to give the reader some idea of how to respond constructively to adolescence as a developmental stage and to troubled adolescents in particular.

This book contains portions of actual case histories. Names, circumstances, and descriptions have been altered to protect the identity and anonymity of those individuals discussed. However, essential elements of the cases are unchanged.

Some of the case examples have been shortened for the purposes of presenting material in the context of this book. Psychotherapy and counseling is in most cases a laborious and arduous process. Occasionally, however, breakthroughs of a brief nature do occur. I have drawn from my years in the helping professions to present several case examples to illustrate complex and important points.

Many of the convincing research findings are repeated throughout the book. This is intentional and is planned to aid the reader in gaining a true comprehension of important material. The questions and exercises at the conclusion of each chapter are not intended to be exhaustive. Their purpose is to stimulate personal thought, reflection, and interpersonal discussion.

My philosophy and ideas as a psychotherapist are influenced by a number of significant people. I doubt that anything I do and little I say as a psychotherapist, speaker, or in any other capacity is original. My style and responses to clinical cases reflect my values and training. There are many people I have learned from, and I certainly cannot name them all here. The most significant figures in my education and training background include Dr. Ed Green; Dr. Gerald Colvin; the late Dr. Clinton Phillips, who originally introduced me to the challenges and creativity of family therapy; Dr. Ed Cox and the entire staff of California Family Study Center; the influence of the late Dr. Milton Erikson through professional training with him as well as continued training with Stephen and Carol Lankton after Dr. Erikson's death; Dr. Doug Carl of Atlanta Institute of Family Studies; and my colleague Dr. Ross Campbell of Southeastern Counseling Center. I have learned much more than I can describe from each of those people and am deeply indebted to them. Their collective influence on me is reflected in the interactions I have daily with clients as well as those found within this book.

I do not consider myself an expert or an author. I am writing this book, first, because I think it needs to be written. To emphasize that point, I think it is essential that the book is written, and as I am sure my father would say if he were alive, "Just do it—somebody needs to!" If I have one redeeming quality, it is that I care deeply.

There have been many people who have loved me and helped shape my life. First and foremost is my wife and coauthor.

My mother has been an incredible friend and mentor through pain and joy. We have a mutual understanding of each other that transcends love. She has consistently presented an example of religious faith in the face of all adversity. My father's influence, although brief because of his premature death, was nonetheless powerful. And then there are all of those who "raised me." They include: my grandfather and grandmother, from whom I learned about the depth love can reach; Rev. Jim Murray; Rev. Barret Gilmer and his wife, Dudley, who probably had a greater influence on me than any one family in my entire life; the late Rev. Joe McLeod and his wife, Virginia, who will never realize what they meant to me during my adolescence; and my stepfather, the late Jack Smith. I loved each of them deeply. Out of their concern they all took me in at various times during my adolescence and made me part of their lives. Only while doing the research for this book did I grow to appreciate what they did and how important it was.

I thank each of them for saving my life.

Why are you in despair, O my soul?
And why have you become disturbed within me?
Hope in God, for I shall again praise Him
For the help of His presence.
O my God, my soul is in despair within me;
    Therefore I remember Thee from the land of the Jordan,
    And the peaks of Hermon, from Mount Mizar.
Deep calls to deep at the sound of Thy waterfalls;
    All of Thy breakers and Thy waves have rolled over me.
    The Lord will command His lovingkindness in the
    daytime;
    And His song will be with me in the night,
    A prayer to the God of my life.

(Psalm 42:5-8)

"... and then from nowhere
    I hear a strange sound
    that doesn't belong
    and can't be found.
A deep call from within,
it's from inside of me.
    It's satan's touch,
    he breathes excitedly. . . .

. . . now I know it's time to die
    and what has happened
    is not a lie.
    The beast leans over
    to take me to death.
    Satan's deep call
is heard under his breath. . . ."

(Sent to me by the mother of
a suicide victim. Written two
days before her daughter's
death in December 1981.)

For this is the message which you have heard from the beginning, that we should love one another. . . . Little children, let us not love with word or with tongue, but in deed and truth.

—John 3:11, 18

Tolerance is the only real test of civilization.

—Arthur Helps

1

THE PROBLEMS OF ADOLESCENT DEPRESSION AND SUICIDE

THE ORIGINS OF PAIN

By my tenth birthday, my parents had been separated for a few months and their divorce was near. I had lost my former zest for life. Life had only recently become so lethargic. My grades had been high but began dropping. I was a playful youngster with many friends but had lost interest in them. Until age ten I had been a healthy, funloving boy who was excited about life. But in my mind all that had changed because of the dissolution of my family.

Fights with my mother followed. I became angry with my grandparents and tried to start trouble with them. My grandfather somehow seemed to understand what was going on. He would let me fume and then reassure me that he loved me. My sister, three years older than I, fought daily with me. That, too, was unusual for our family.

I tried to figure what I could have done to make things better. *If I would have done this—or hadn't done that—perhaps*

the divorce was my fault, I would think. I felt split between
my parents and didn't want to hurt their feelings. But
there was no way out of it, in my ten-year-old mind. No
matter whom I lived with, someone would get hurt. Living
currently with my grandfather was a way to avoid hurting
either parent, but that could not continue forever.

I was looking forward to my father's visit. He was coming home from California to take me on vacation. We
would have time alone. It was a special season, and I
looked forward to it with the joy only a ten-year-old could
possibly anticipate.

That night we had not expected mother to visit. She
appeared at the front door accompanied by several of her
friends. There was a sudden blur of activity. Things began
to run together in my mind. Someone began to scream,
and someone else cried. It even seems someone fainted. I
was only able to piece together fragments here and there.
Confusion and fear began to build. I searched out my
grandfather and asked him what was wrong. He took me
in his arms and through his tears explained that my father
had been killed.

I don't remember all that happened afterward or how it
evolved. Some small amount of time passed. I recall the
disbelief and demands I made. Nobody at that age wants
to accept the death of a parent. But if it was true, then I
too would die!

I ran into my grandmother's kitchen and pulled out a
large butcher knife. I wrapped my fingers around the
handle, lifted the knife toward my chest and began to stab
myself. It seemed logical at the time. I would join my
father and spend eternity with him. For some reason I felt
no pain as the knife entered my side. A scream came from
within me, although I didn't recognize my own voice. I
recall my grandfather wrapping his strong arms around
me. I began to sob almost convulsively as he held me to his
chest. My body jerked as I slowly lost consciousness.

Then I slept.

I survived.

The impact of that experience, however, lives with me.
I'm certain it affects the way I relate to life today.

A SURVEY OF THE PROBLEM

During the winter of 1984 I saw a problem developing in my hometown of Chattanooga. Our counseling center offices were experiencing an inordinate number of adolescents in serious stages of depression. We were hearing daily about suicides and suicide attempts. My colleague and close friend Dr. Ross Campbell had discussed this on several occasions and agreed that "something" was quite wrong.

On February 25 I received a phone call from a local high school principal. There had been two student suicides and several other attempts at his school within a three-week period. That afternoon and several days thereafter, I spent a great deal of time with the principal and a group of teachers discussing teenage depression and suicide. I was shocked by the nature of the task that I had taken on and grew convinced that something else of a larger nature had to be done. I returned to my office to find that the secretarial staff had rescheduled my regular appointments to make room for emergencies. The same thing had occurred with other professionals on the staff. Teenagers were being admitted to psychiatric facilities so quickly that there were no longer any vacancies. Several local facilities had developed a waiting list. The public agencies that specialized in adolescent treatment were all filled.

On February 26 Dr. Campbell and I decided we had to do something of a larger nature. A public response needed to be made. Acting individually we could not solve the crisis. It was going to have to include the efforts of others.

The story of how our response developed is explained in chapter 13. The effort culminated when a capacity crowd attended a public symposium. Unfortunately, between February 26, when I had the original idea, and May 14, when the symposium was held, national statistics indicate approximately 6,300 Americans committed suicide. Additionally, approximately 70,000 adolescents attempted suicide during that same period.

A CASE OF ADOLESCENT SUICIDE

Tom and Jeanette were convinced they loved each other. They had been sure for quite some time. Curiously enough the two had met in their fifth-grade Sunday school class. They started dating in the seventh grade and had shared an exclusive dating relationship since then.

Both were somewhat quiet and had few friends. What friends they did have described Tom and Jeanette as absorbed, moody, and often depressed. Their friends didn't want to associate with them. In Tom's and Jeanette's minds, that didn't matter. There was no need for friends because Tom and Jeanette met so many of each other's social needs. Those needs they were unable to meet soon began to be ignored. Other friendships that did exist also began to evaporate from lack of attention, and the two were driven even closer together.

Tom and Jeanette lived in upper middle-class suburbs. Their parents were professionals, attended church regularly, and generally were active members of society. They loved their children very much but didn't demonstrate their love freely. There was a great deal of "healthy" pressure put on the children to excel in school and in their personal lives. Neither parent seemed to object to the dating relationship that developed speedily between the two teenagers.

Dating endured through the high school years. They attended the same classes, visited Sunday school and church services together, and sometimes shared meals with each other's families. Their parents had privately discussed the direction of their teenagers' relationship. Tom's former friends saw him withdrawing further. Jeanette's grades fell over the next few months. Tom ultimately lost interest in athletics and quit the soccer team, where he had previously excelled. His grades also began to drop.

Finally, Tom's parents confronted him about the amount of time he was spending with Jeanette. The encounter developed into a fight with no positive outcome. A second discussion ended as negatively. Similar meetings had transpired between Jeanette and her parents. With accelerated pressure forced by the parents, the couple's relationship flourished even more. They banded together intimately in defiance of their parents.

To the teenagers, marriage seemed to be the only possible alternative, although they knew their parents would not allow it. In fact, by this point, Jeanette's parents had refused to allow her to date Tom. She convinced Tom that if she became pregnant, they would certainly be allowed to marry. After all, neither of their parents agreed with abortion. It made sense to them.

She didn't know that at that very moment she was indeed well over two months pregnant. When her parents shortly thereafter discovered it, they sent her to a home for unwed mothers several hundred miles away and refused Tom the right to see her. The child would be put up for adoption. At that point, both Tom's and Jeanette's parents forbade them to visit each other.

Saturday night, following two unsuccessful weeks of attempting to contact Jeanette, Tom took his own life with his father's 12-gauge shotgun. Jeanette heard about his death one month later when she returned home after a miscarriage. She joined him in death by taking a drug overdose.

The above scenario was real. It happened as depicted and has probably been repeated time and again. Teen suicides similar to Tom and Jeanette's occur nearly 6,000 times per year in our country.

THE SCOPE OF TEENAGE SUICIDE

Dr. Seymour Perlin, board chairman of the National Youth Suicide Center in Washington, D.C., has stated publicly that approximately 2 million people between the ages of thirteen and nineteen will attempt suicide each year. The National Institute of Mental Health suggests that approximately 30,000 people will successfully take their own lives annually through a variety of means. That is nearly 1 person every twenty minutes or more than 70 persons per day!

It is difficult to determine the number of those that are Christians. The fact is that the problem does exist in the Christian community.

Suicide is the second-leading cause of death among teenagers. The rate has tripled in the last twenty years, and the actual toll is likely much higher. Many deaths are probably either disguised or listed as accidents, when they may well have been self-inflicted.

One interesting trend that has recently developed is the *cluster phenomenon*. Other people have termed it "copy cat suicide." However it is labeled, the phenomenon is an alarming one. Clustering is the propensity of suicides to occur in groups.

One expert recently stated that suicides never occur singularly. He suggested they always occur in groups of two or more. This has been illustrated nationwide. The most well-reported clusters have occurred outside of large cities in affluent, upper and upper-middle-class suburbs. The possible reasons for that will be discussed in a later chapter. The purpose of mentioning the clusters here is to illustrate the problem.

In Chattanooga there were nine reported suicides within a four-month period. This was in a city with a population of only 175,000. As mentioned earlier, two of those suicides were teenagers from the same high school. In another episode, two people leaped from local bridges into the Tennessee River within two hours of each other. Several nights later a young female college student survived a similar leap.

Behavioral epidemiologists have kept records of this nature for quite some time. For whatever reason, clusters do exist, and it is a well-accepted fact that suicides occur in group patterns. Perhaps the fact of one person's taking his or her life makes it less of a violation to a second or third person. The epidemiologists also tell us that divorces and other emotional problems occur in similar clusters.

A growing number of communities have been devastated by suicide clusters. Among them are suburbs of Dallas, Houston, Chicago, Washington, D.C., and New York City. Those areas have several factors in common. Obviously they are all close to major cities. Each suburban area has a high emphasis on upper social mobility and is quite wealthy. They are all predominantly populated with white middle-class families and a highly transient population. There is an absence of extended family relationships and, in more than one case, an absence of senior citizens. As is the case nationwide, there is also a high divorce rate and a larger number of single-parent families. As will be mentioned in future chapters, all of those factors seem to be important indicators of stress for adolescents and adults as well.

There is no single explanation to the problem of increased suicides. Many have tried to explain, and various answers have been offered. None are sufficient. It is an understatement to say the source of the problem is as complex as modern American society itself.

THE HURRIED SOCIETY

Adolescents today do indeed face a more difficult life than any past generation. The change in technology alone has presented teenagers with a multitude of problems and opportunities most adults have never faced. As a society we probably have also sanctioned a value on growing up rapidly. Many have referred to this as "the hurried society" phenomenon.

Basically we are forcing our children to grow up too fast. As an example, I have seen parents of five- or six-year-olds screaming angrily at their children during soccer matches to improve the performance of their children in some way. The response of the youngster is always a combination of embarrassment, withdrawal, and confusion. This often begins an anger cycle in the child, which will be discussed in more detail later. That sort of public pressure is inappropriate even for a teenager. The effect on a child of five or six years could be devastating.

One of my favorite examples of the "hurry up and grow up" mentality is a popular merchandising catalog. There are pictures of seven- and eight-year-old girls dressed and made up to appear older. I cut out one particular picture and at random asked several of my friends to guess her age. The responses were seventeen years old, eighteen years old, and sixteen years old. One friend, who happens to be a professional model, said it was an eleven-year-old girl trying to look like an eighteen-year-old. Actually, she was seven.

The hurried society encourages children to hurry and grow up. Obviously, physical changes can be hurried or

faked. Even certain biochemical changes can be hastened
along. For instance, the average age of the onset of men-
struation has changed from twenty in 1880 to approximately eleven today. An adolescent can easily develop a
mature vocabulary, a mature walk, and a mature body.
Similar to the picture of the seven-year-old girl, appearances can be deceiving and can be altered substantially.
However, emotional maturity cannot be so easily faked.

Some children are being forced to fake it. During a
counseling session with a twelve-year-old boy, we discussed
his fears. This is a rather routine kind of discussion during
counseling, even for a twelve-year-old. Without hesitation,
he stated that his most crushing fear was not being a
success in business. I was shocked. A twelve-year-old boy is
not emotionally equipped to deal with that kind of issue. I
recall I had fears at age twelve. But none of them had to
do with being a success in business.

Today's teens are forced to make decisions quickly. It is
estimated most children by the age of ten will have had the
opportunity to use drugs. They are forced to be careful
that they aren't "stolen" by one of their parents or someone else. Another sobering estimate is that nearly 75 to 80
percent of teenagers are dropping out of formal church
attendance. Many times I see the roles of parent and child
reversed as a young teenager comforts a divorced parent
and assures him that things will work out. Adolescents are
victims of sexual and physical abuse more than at any time
in the history of our nation. And the emotional response
of teens I deal with daily reflects it. The hurried society
creates stress and pressures teenagers simply are not
equipped to handle.

We ask our teenagers to mature beyond their emotional
capacity. This leads to dissonance and a condition of dis-
harmony within the child. Often it results in anger, which
we as adults don't want to accept. If we don't allow the
adolescent to express the anger, it can take many other
forms, including depression, juvenile delinquincy, or rebellious behavior. Any of those responses, if not dealt with
properly, can eventually evolve into a suicide crisis. The
problem is indeed complex.

As a young adolescent, after my father's death, I moved

in with my grandparents for an extended period of time. My grandfather was a farmer, and we all worked extremely hard. After the day was over, I would play on the front porch of their home. Later, my grandmother would come out and sit in her rocking chair. I would look up and ask how she was doing. She would smile at me, pause for a moment, and then respond.

"I'm plumb give out, Johnny—plumb give out!"

I think my grandmother was saying that she was tired and had given just about all she had. In many ways, that is how I see our adolescents.

They are, indeed, "plumb give out."

FOR FURTHER THOUGHT

1. Describe a period of time during which you were close to being severely depressed and/or suicidal. Who or what intervened and helped preserve your life?

2. Examine how you deal with the hurried society today. Do you seek out a friend or relative to discuss your stress? Do you wait for someone to notice your mood changes? Is it easy or hard to work through the distress? How does it compare with the way you used to cope?

3. Notice the frequency of your discouraged periods. What events or situations occur just before or surrounding them? What triggers discouragement for you? How long do periods of discouragement last? Think of any patterns to your periods of discouragement.

4. Consider whether members of your family or friends have or had problems with depression. How does their depression affect you?

5. How do teenagers respond to you during your periods of discouragement? What are you teaching them with regard to coping with discouragement? Are you model-

ing for them an example that will help them learn how to effectively cope with their own discouragement?

6. Think of someone you know who may have attempted suicide or strongly considered it. Analyze his behavior prior to the attempt. Do you now notice any patterns?

To everything there is a season, and a time to every purpose under the heaven.

—Ecclesiastes 3:1, KJV*

Oftentimes the test of courage becomes rather to live than to die.

—Vittorio Alfieri, *Ovestes*

*King James Version.

2

THE NATURE OF ADOLESCENCE

INTRODUCTION

O f life's various transitions, perhaps none is more confusing and occasionally traumatic as adolescence. This is probably not surprising, as the period is known as one of intense change. Rapid physical growth, intellectual development, psycho-social maturity, and dozens of legal changes all occur in a brief span of time. The frustration teens experience is matched only by that of parents.

"OUT OF THE MOUTHS OF BABES . . ."

"He was a perfect child. He never did anything wrong. You couldn't ask for a better kid—you know what I am saying? I mean, we expected a lot from him, but it all seemed to come so easy. When he turned fifteen it was as if somebody had just flipped a switch."

The mother's eyes began to fill with tears as she sat and gazed toward the floor. Her husband and son regarded her protectively. I waited silently and gazed at the same spot on the floor she did, as if the answer was to be found there. The silence expanded awkwardly as her husband began to clear his throat several times.

"He has changed a lot," her husband said to no one in particular. "Sometimes it is as if we don't know him—."

"Tom,"—I looked toward the teenager—"I hear your parents referring to you a great deal but not speaking to you. Is there any comment you want to make to them?"

Tom returned my gaze for a few moments without answering. Then he began to speak almost haltingly.

"Sure—I didn't know I was supposed to be—the same as I was four or five years ago. I mean—after all—I am growing up. Right?"

Silence.

His father was the first to begin laughing. The laugh built to a roar.

Then Tom began giggling.

After a few seconds mother and then I finally joined them.

"Out of the mouths of babes . . ."

ADOLESCENCE DEFINED

Tom was right in both his definition and the implications. Fifteen-year-olds are supposed to be growing up. And it is an exceptionally stormy, painful process for many. It is made even more problematic by us as parents forgetting our own teen years. That is a very easy thing to do, but nonetheless damaging. It can also be destructive to the delicate communication link between parent and child.

Several years ago I was visiting my mother and sisters in another city. At the time, my sister had a teenage son who was experiencing some of the normal yet nearly intolerable changes most adolescents go through. My mother expressed exasperation with her grandson's behavior.

She explained that it "just didn't make any sense." I reminded her of my problems at that age and, in my nephew's behalf, described what he experienced as relatively normal.

That bit of advice didn't seem to help my mother at all. After several minutes of discussion, her frustration was clarified. The problem she was having had to do with the developmental variability faced by adolescents. A teen can progress at one speed on a particular level and at a totally different speed on another level. My nephew was experiencing that paradox. It didn't make sense to my mother that a teenager could walk around with a "lollipop in his mouth and sex on his mind!" He was at one developmental stage socially and another emotionally.

We all laughed at her characterization. It is indeed humorous, but one of the most poetically accurate descriptions I have heard. Adolescence is puzzling to both adults and teenagers. The paradox my mother described represents the dichotomies, confusion, and frustration faced during these years by adolescents and adults alike.

TRANSITION

Adolescence is a period of tremendous transition. More transformation occurs during this time than during the rest of our lives put together. As explained above, it is made even more burdensome because of the inconsistency and multitude of changes. The transitions occur at various paces and levels. A teenager can have the physical appearance of an adult but the cognitive capacities of a child. Or a teen can possess the social skills of someone twice his age and still be an emotional toddler. Those various dichotomies occur seldom with such polarity anywhere else during life. However, they flourish during the adolescent years.

The dilemma of adolescence is nowhere more obvious than with the "experts" when they try to define it. Some people refer to the period of adolescence as an adaptation to puberty. However, often puberty (a biological and chemical change) begins at a late age, long after the teen has begun to behave and think of himself as an adolescent (a social change). Others attempt to attach some chronological age span to the period. Depending on the source, this can vary, beginning at ages ten or eleven and lasting anywhere up to ages eighteen through twenty-four. That span is quite wide and fairly representative of the disagreement, even among the experts. Others define adolescence merely as that period that encompasses the process of change occurring between childhood and adulthood. In that sense, adolescence bridges the gap between childhood and adulthood. For the purposes of this book, the terms *adolescent, teenager,* and *child* will be used interchangeably. They all will refer to the transition period as described above.

HISTORICAL PERSPECTIVE

It is interesting to consider that adolescence is a creation of man, not God. Until recently, children were not granted the transitional period. Historically, the children were viewed as miniature adults.

The trend recently has been toward an increased period of adolescence. As the life span has lengthened over the years, there has been an equal extension of the period we generally have come to refer to and define as adolescence. Considering what teens face during that interval, both bodily and socially, it is appropriate for the time to extend even longer.

An interesting trend has been the appearance of a second transitional term, *youth,* which practically lengthens adolescence. Youth have been considered postadolescent, yet still not quite adults. This group can often be found living in apartment complexes, spending substantial time in socializing, hobbies, and dating before taking on the responsibilities of a family. The single youth trend is one that is growing and presents an interesting study of postadolescent development.

BODILY CHANGES

Anatomical, physiological, and biochemical changes occur during the teen years. Those are referred to as bodily transformations. The production of various hormones by the endocrine glands results in an unbelievably rapid period of change. Some transitions are rather obvious but perhaps personal. Dramatic alterations occur in both male and female adolescents. Voices change. Females' breasts begin developing. Facial and body hair begins to appear. The genitals change shape, size, and sometimes color. There is usually a growth spurt during this period, and the adolescent will often appear awkward, both physically and socially.

Some biochemical changes can lead to emotionally upsetting experiences with no apparent source. In females, these can alter the regularity of the menstrual cycle or effect other confusing occurrences. Hormonal variances of this nature can make the adolescent act and feel differently. Sometimes new drives are produced that the adolescent has never experienced.

Those collective changes create confusion and frustration. Often the frustration is mistaken by adults as rebelliousness. Biochemical fluctuations are neither regular nor cyclic. Their unpredictability in both male and female adolescents is an added factor that makes the nature of adolescence so stressful.

INTELLECTUAL CHANGES

The early childhood years are marked by a preoccupation with what the great Swiss scientist Jean Piaget identified as "concrete thinking." This is a term describing the inclination of the child to experience life in somewhat rigid terms. Reality is viewed in an "either/or," "black/white" frame of reference. Little room is granted for nuance or shades of difference. Thinking symbolically (or figuratively) is still beyond their capability. Life is interpreted literally, or at face value.

During adolescence the capacity for more abstract thought patterns emerges. The young person becomes more capable of dealing creatively with hypothetical thought. Accompanying this development is the characteristic pattern of questioning and sometimes even challenging authority. This is basically a normal and healthy process as the adolescent begins to sort out reality in his or her own terms instead of passively accepting the inherited frame of reference.

Those adolescents with more creative and imaginative minds often experience the most difficulty during this period. They find themselves questioning all sources of established authority and even recommending better ways. Those sources can include the legal structure, government, and obviously the family. At times it may seem to the parents that this child is rebellious or oppositional about everything. In such cases, extra measures of patience and support are necessary while the child struggles with this important phase of intellectual exploration.

SPIRITUAL CHANGES

Naturally, during this period, the adolescent may also challenge or question the religious authority he is placed under. Specifically, this may lead to some becoming disillusioned with formalities of the church, the teachings of Christ, or the authority of the Bible. The goal of parents needs to be to point their children in a direction of spiritual redefinition, that is, a refocusing of their religious faith.

Spiritual redefinition is the process of encouraging the adolescent to redefine and refocus his religious faith, that is, his faith in God. In essence, it is the point of view that encourages the teen to become responsible for his own personal relationship with God. The focus is then centered toward a one-to-one relationship of adolescent to God rather than the triangle of adolescent through parent to God.

During early years a child's faith is most dependent on the exposure parents provide. As the infant grows into adolescence and begins to experience abstract reasoning, questions will arise concerning spiritual matters and faith in God. Sometimes a teenager will decide his parents' convictions are insufficient. Depending on the adolescent, he may either ignore religion, become discouraged, or even attempt to drop out of formal religious activity. Other times it can be a turning point for the teen. This aspect of development can be one of the most difficult of challenges for parents.

All teenagers will come to this point as a matter of basic growth. It is vital, natural, and inevitable. Encouraging such a redefinition or refocus will often prevent the adolescent from totally rejecting Christianity. Experience seems to prove, in any case, that parents cannot "force feed" a particular belief to their children.

The reassuring point is to realize that all of adolescence is a transitional process. Maturing spiritually also requires transition. Sometimes, that transition may be difficult. However, parents have already set a foundation of growth by this time. It is expected that the teen will vary from the foundation somewhat. However, the psalmist assures that "a tree firmly planted" will remain fruitful (Psalm 1:3).

GENDER ROLE CHANGES

In modern American society there is a trend toward what some sociologists call *androgyny*. Androgyny is the term used to describe a tendency to blend traditionally male and female characteristics. Sociologists observe adolescents today taking the more adaptive or useful traits from both the traditional role stereotypes for male and female and rejecting those traits that are maladaptive or harmful. This seems to be a real trend, and some suggest a healthy one. Most psychologists and sociologists recognize that certain traditional male traits such as stoicism and the inability to express emotions can create problems. Likewise, some traditional female characteristics such as being overly emotional and helpless can create equal problems. Generally speaking, the current adolescent generation is much healthier and adaptive than past generations. And, in spite of tradition, today's young people show greater maturity in cultivating the more useful characteristics of both genders.

However, traditional gender roles still exist. For males, that role involves a primary responsibility of establishing dominance over the environment. For females, the role remains a more sensitive nurturing relationship that still includes the primary responsibility for child-rearing. Although there may not be an instinctual movement toward these roles, it is safe to say from historical, social, and spiritual perspectives that they will continue to occur. So even though society changes, and in spite of a trend toward androgyny, traditional gender roles are still accepted.

DEVELOPMENTAL INCONSISTENCY

It is accurate to describe the psychological and social changes as reflecting the transition from the dependent child to the independent adult. This trend is a strong one that leads to innumerable inconsistencies, paradoxes, and often confusion. This confusion is also apparent at times within the legal structure.

I am reminded of my own adolescence when at age eighteen I was mature enough to go to Vietnam, get wounded, and later almost killed. However, apparently I was not considered mature enough to vote in local or national elections. When I returned from combat duty in Vietnam, a former friend was very critical of me for fighting for our country when I could not vote. After considering the dichotomy, I was quite puzzled about how to respond.

That same kind of disparity is reflected daily as parents and adolescents collide in the movement toward independence. Seldom do any of the parties fully understand the dynamics of what is actually occurring. However, when viewed from a transitional viewpoint it becomes more clear.

PARENTING GOALS

The goal of parenting could probably be defined in a variety of ways. However, it would have to include some element of rearing mature, responsible young people who possess a healthy set of moral values and will someday make a contribution to society and their own families. This process begins at birth and probably never ends. However, the ending begins when a child leaves home. Leaving home begins the day an infant becomes a toddler and is completed the day the young adult says good-bye and drives away never to return. However, the process is most intense during adolescence. It is the developmental equivalent of cramming for the final exam.

The period is often stormy for both parent and teen. The young person is experiencing a multitude of changes, occurring so rapidly that it is almost impossible to keep up. The focus becomes internal as the teen tries to understand these changes. This leads to intellectual and social stress. Parents often don't seem to understand, so the teenager turns to peers who are experiencing similar confusion. In the midst of all these internal and family crises, the adolescent is asked to make totally unrealistic decisions relating to the distant future.

My nephew, at the age of fourteen and going through his own adolescent transition, had to make a decision that would affect the rest of his life. He was forced to decide if he would take college preparatory, general education, or vocational courses in high school. That may seem a small decision, but in many parts of the country a student cannot attend college unless he has taken college preparatory courses in high school. Thus, a person may be prevented from pursuing a career that requires a college education merely because he has made an impulsive decision at age thirteen or fourteen.

There are literally hundreds of similar examples. Society has many unrealistic expectations that are presented to teenagers. Teens are forced to make one of the most important decisions they will ever make at the worst possible time of their lives. This expectation ignores the fact that most thirteen-year-olds are incapable of making such a decision to begin with. Yet a major source of authority (the school) presents the teenager with this responsibility.

Needless to say, parents have a responsibility to assist the teenager carefully in making such weighty decisions.

IDENTITY FORMATION

During the period of rapid and intense change, society introduces new pressures to the teenager. And, as if that were not enough, an added ingredient occurs. The teen begins to experience need for a sense of separate identity.

We all have a need to define ourselves and be able to explain that "this is who I am." This has been defined as either a conscious or unconscious sense of individual uniqueness. Identity is a vitally important process and necessary to later emotional stability. However, some adults (and often understandably so) have the least patience during this critical time. Quite often adults reach burnout by simply being loving and nurturing parents.

It is encouraging that once this identity formation is complete, the adolescent finds himself relating maturely to the parents. This is often initially detected by the parent even before the adolescent. It can appear as quickly as the "switch that was flipped" at the beginning of the chapter.

One of the greatest factors needed during the identity formation is adult relationships. In male children, there is an absolute necessity for adult male attention. This can be with the father figure or some other significant adult male. With boys, more than girls, there is this need for adult attention from figures other than parents. Obviously a need exists for maternal and other adult female attention. However, the need for nonsexual adult male attention among adolescent boys is strongest. It is also vital.

Female adolescents usually identify more closely with their mothers, if that relationship is a good one. If not, they will often search out a surrogate figure. Attention from adult males is also necessary for healthy identity formation in females, but not as vital as it is with boys. Affection of a nonsexual nature from adult men will usually lead to an increased sense of self-worth for the adolescent female.

For adolescents to have a healthy identity formation process, they must have high self-esteem. This ultimately requires their liking themselves for who they are. In a later chapter we will discuss the self-esteem connection.

THE PROCESS OF IDENTITY

It has been implied that perhaps some people never reach a true identity formation. It is also equally theorized that this formation is necessary if a person is ever going to reach intimacy with another. Simply put, before we can like someone else enough to become intimate, we must like ourselves. That point of view is supported scripturally. Christ indicated that the second most important commandment is: "Love thy neighbor as thyself." This is second only to loving "the Lord thy God with all your heart, . . . soul, and . . . mind" (Matthew 22:37–39).

It would seem difficult to love your neighbor if you did not first love yourself. If that is not true, then we run into a philosophical quandary. If I must love my neighbor as myself, and I dislike myself, then in what way am I going to love my neighbor? It is impossible to love my neighbor if I dislike myself. If I dislike myself, I can only dislike my neighbor.

To put it another way, you cannot give away that which you don't own. If I don't own five dollars, I cannot give someone else five dollars. Similarly, if I don't own love, I cannot give it away. And to own love, I must first love myself.

This is the significance of identity formation. It is vital for adolescents to reach the point where they are comfortable with who they are. If they are not comfortable, perhaps further self-esteem growth needs to occur to help them reach that point.

This growth can come from a variety of sources. Perhaps the child is lacking in personal depth or experience. The difficulty could be found instead in the lack of social relationships with either parents, other adults, or peers. Or possibly the source of strain lies in the absence of a spiritual redefinition.

SOCIAL CHANGES

International travelers often experience a phenomenon some refer to as culture shock. Culture shock occurs when one is taken from a highly industrialized or technological society and placed in a society that is less developed, or vice versa. An example of this might be a missionary who leaves a large urban U.S. airport on one day and two days later arrives by foot in a jungle outpost in another country. The dramatic disparity in cultures can leave the missionary almost in a state of shock. Many years ago, author Alvin Toffler wrote *Future Shock*. One of the many implications of that outstanding book was that society changes so rapidly that we have difficulty adapting to it. The experience can be compared to the missionary described above.

Today, teenagers face a monumental amount of social change and an unhealthy abundance of information. We are at times engulfed with that, even as adults. In many cases, teenagers literally live in a state of shock. The unbelievable kinds of changes and the tempo of their occurrence is simply more than they can cope with.

In chapter 1, the concept of the hurried society was discussed. Social change is one component of that concept. It contributes to the environmental confusion that our internally confused teenagers face. The antidote may be stability.

If the adolescent is presented with a stable family and religious community, the odds of depression and suicide are probably decreased. The family unit can provide the intensity and nurture needed for healthy emotional development, whereas the church can provide an extended network of family and social relationships and an avenue for a closer relationship with God.

All indicators are that those sources could ease the transition that makes the nature of adolescence one of confusion and difficulty.

FOR FURTHER THOUGHT

1. Recall times in your life when your family didn't seem to understand you. How did you deal with them? What qualities helped? From you? From your family?

2. List the most significant adults in your adolescent period. Explain what it was about those people that made their relationships important.

3. Make notes of the words or actions of significant adults that you recall as being most helpful to you.

4. Who are the most significant people in your life today other than your immediate family? What attributes do those people have that make them important to you?

5. Think of the qualities and characteristics you listed in the above questions. Which of those do you have to offer to others, including teenagers?

Be gracious to me, O Lord, for I am in distress; my eye is wasted away from grief, my soul and my body also. For my life is spent with sorrow.

—Psalm 31:9–10

The pain of the mind is worse than the pain of the body.

—Syrius

3

ADOLESCENT STRESS

A CASE OF FAMILY DISTRESS

Ted's parents had divorced eighteen months earlier. I visited with him and his mother three weeks after his father had remarried. Ted reacted in family therapy as any depressed adolescent. He sat, stared at the floor, and seldom responded in any way other than shrugging his shoulders or nodding his head. His mother spoke with great animation when she told how Ted had almost broken her nose during an argument. Many arguments they had experienced occurred immediately after visiting with his father, so Ted's mother had limited that visitation. Ted had not seen his father in several months at the time of our first visit. Passively, he stated it would be nice to visit his father.

During the next two sessions it became evident that Ted's behavior had begun to deteriorate at home. However, he was growing verbal in the sessions. One night he had stayed out until 3:00 A.M. against his mother's wishes. On another occasion he had refused to attend school. But he was becoming more active in counseling and expressing himself quite well.

At a subsequent session, Ted stated that his behavior was the result of anger. He was angry both at his father and his mother. However, he didn't openly object to the limits his mother had imposed on him.

On somewhat of an impulse I turned to the mother and explained that Ted was honoring her limits on his visitation primarily out of loyalty to her.

"He loves you very much and doesn't want to hurt your feelings. But you have to pay a high price for that kind of loyalty. He knows you experience pain, especially since the remarriage of your former husband. But punishing your husband by limiting his visitation is only hurting Ted. He'll go along with you and not press to visit. He'll cooperate because he is angry with his father, too. But you're going to pay a price. If he is not allowed to visit his dad, problems will just increase."

"That's absurd," she shouted. "That's stupid! I'm not trying to punish anybody. I'm glad he got married. I am glad—it's finally over. It's over! It's finally—."

Mrs. Smith stopped in mid-sentence and began to shake rhythmically as she fought back the tears that begged to fall. When she finally erupted, the months of suppressed grief came out volcanically. Ted joined her as they openly wept for the first time at the dissolution of their family.

WHAT IS STRESS?

Stress is something we experience continuously. In fact, some people say that a day without stress is death. It occurs every time we experience change. It also occurs when we are forced to deal with something we perceive as threatening or something we perceive simply as being new.

Those things that are new can be perceived as either positive or negative. A strained relationship can be stressful. Yet a promotion or successful relationship can also lead to stress. That is especially true if it is a significant change. The stress that creates problems is that which leads to a chronic state of distress. Such distress can occur as a result of cumulative stress over a period of time. Or it can occur as a result of one or two major events.

In the example discussed above, Ted and his mother were responding to several different traumatic factors. Facing them was family dissolution, family reorganization, adjustment to financial changes, the remarriage of Ted's father, and denial of grief. Ted had begun responding to his own level of distress by anger outbursts and other behavioral problems.

FIGHT OR FLIGHT

The basic human response to stress has been described as the "fight or flight" mechanism. In the face of distress, the body prepares itself to either fight or flee the enemy. This is an old response and one that is probably useful during a time of threat or danger. The body basically gears itself for combat. Unfortunately, as a result of modern society's pace, we have generalized the response to situations that don't require it. In some people, "fight or flight" occurs twice daily during rush-hour traffic. This is one reason the concept of stress is so widely discussed today.

Stress can cause anxiety and fear, digestive problems, hypertension, fatigue, sleeping difficulties, inability to concentrate, and many other complications. Intense stress has been linked to heart attacks, alcoholism and other drug addiction, and even to cancer.

The American family has been one of the true victims of stress. Reciprocally, the deterioration of the American family has increased the amount of stress that must be dealt with by the adolescent population. The relationship has become cyclic and self-perpetuating. Adolescence has been referred to by some researchers as an age of anxiety. That is an appropriate description, considering the enormous number of trying issues being faced during this time.

ADOLESCENT STRESS DEFINED

There are volumes of material written about stress. However, most of the material is directed toward adults. Adolescents experience stress in a similar manner. Yet some experiences that would introduce no stress to an adult can be devastating to a teenager. Because of the nature of adolescence, identity formation is still in a critically unstable condition. Any stress, therefore, will probably be experienced more intensely by an adolescent and be more unbalancing.

SOCIAL NETWORK AND PERSONALITY RESOURCES

Each adolescent has certain personality resources that enable him to deal with life to some degree. Those resources are composed of a variety of factors. A teen's personality strength is predominantly a result of several key factors. Those factors begin with the strength of the interpersonal relationships within the family of origin.

Other factors include establishment of a strong identity; the ability to deal with anger and other strong emotions; a presence of hope or optimism; a strong spiritual relationship; the condition of his self-esteem; extended family network; and adaptation to school and other social institutions.

However, clearly the most important consideration is strong family relationships. The family can provide the teen with a stable foundation for cultivating additional relationships with both peers and other significant adults. Without a wide variety of relationships in any of those categories mentioned above, personality resources will be quite shallow and superficial. Thus, the adolescent's ability to successfully deal with stress may be adversely affected.

A CASE OF LIMITED RESOURCES

Johnny's mother brought him to see me because of what she described as an obsession with guilt. He had complained of a fear of "being possessed" and was convinced he was evil. I discovered that Johnny had a very poor relationship with his father. His father (who attended none of the counseling sessions) was an overworked man and repeatedly showed little patience with his fourteen-year-old son. He was critical of the music Johnny listened to and had recently become irate when he discovered Johnny reading a book on the sexual development of teenagers. The book had been checked out of his local church library and seemed to be quite appropriate and discreet. Yet the father had severely punished Johnny for reading it. Over the past few years, Johnny could only recall confrontations with his father. He did remember quality time with his father, although it had occurred many years earlier. I discussed this with Johnny's father over the telephone. He

explained that because of his responsibilities as a business-
man, he had very little time to spend with his son.

Johnny attended a private Christian school, where he
experienced frustration with the restrictions imposed by
his teacher. Occasionally he was publically punished for
infractions. In Johnny's words, he began to feel that he
was "weird."

The situation was made more complex because Johnny
did not seem to blend in with the other students at the
school. He described himself as having no close friends.
The only person he seemed to be able to talk to was his
mother.

When he began to ask questions and discuss with her his
extreme degree of guilt and fear, she decided to bring him
in for counseling. Johnny confided in me that although he
had considered killing himself at various times, he had not
considered it seriously. He was depressed and experienced
an unhealthy level of guilt and anxiety.

Johnny was immediately placed in another school with a
less rigid system of discipline. He quickly met and began
associating with peers he could talk to. He grew more open
with me and began discussing his thoughts at great length.
He learned that he could also talk to other adults. Within
several sessions there was little evidence of depression, and
Johnny was more energetic and optimistic.

Johnny felt isolated from his father. Because of his father's unwillingness to become involved in counseling, I
was not able to deal with that problem. However, I provided Johnny with a significant male adult to whom he
could relate without being criticized or judged. As he grew
confident in our relationship, he naturally began reaching
out to other adults. Johnny actually was a very mature and
socially skilled youngster. However, he had little confidence. When he began to reach out to other people, they
found him a delightful companion and enjoyed spending
time with him. That in return increased his self-confidence.

When he changed schools, Johnny soon became very
popular and developed a broad social network of both
male and female peers. The previous school had been a
stressful factor that was removed from Johnny's life. Parents
must be certain to observe children's individual responses

to even the best of schools. Sometimes, what seems good to a parent can be devastating to a child.

It is almost impossible to overstate the importance of a healthy social network of adolescent and adult friends. One important ability a parent can teach a child is the opportunity and skills to develop relationships. This process of skill building can begin at birth. A parent can encourage a child as early as the parent is able to communicate with the child. If the foundation can be established during infancy, the adolescent will more likely be able to adapt to the turbulent teenage years. If Johnny's father had been able to spend more quality time with him, the problems would likely have been less critical.

CRISIS AND COPING

Regardless of the resources any of us have available, crises can always occur. During a crisis most people need a special measure of support. The crisis can be great if the adolescent does not have a spiritual mentor to turn to. The counselor does not have to be highly trained but needs to be someone who cares, is willing to listen, and will be supportive.

It is important to realize that something very minor can be a major provocation to a teen. This may be because of the adolescent's incapacity to perceive the nature of a particular event. At other times, the provocation may be because of a friend or sibling problem. Often we may never know the true problem. As adults we may only see the manifestation of the child's refusing to eat, withdrawing to the bedroom, or arguing over absurd matters. At such times we have to look beyond the obvious for clarification. That takes extreme patience and restraint.

At other times the stressful event is quite obvious. Such distinct occurrences provide parents with opportunity to plan in advance and closely observe the child. Usually stressful incidents alone do not result in suicide attempts. However, they can be precipitating factors if the teen is otherwise depressed, angry, or troubled.

DEATH OF A FAMILY MEMBER

Death within the family can be one of the most stressful circumstances to cope with for either adult or adolescent. Basically, however, teens are usually poorly equipped to deal with such a crisis; and at a time when they need parental support, the family is often unable to provide it. It can be wise at this point to introduce an objective person into the family support system. That person can be a clergyman, counselor, pediatrician, or some other sympathetic but emotionally detached figure. The child must be allowed to grieve as long as needed over the death of a family member. Expressing one's emotions freely is much preferred to holding back, particularly with such a major loss.

DEATH OF A FRIEND

A friend's death can be an extremely stressful event. Everything that applies in the section on death of a family member applies here. Parents need to take special precautions, especially if the death was of a best friend. If the death was from suicide or any other violent form, seek professional help immediately. These kinds of deaths nearly always result in depression within surviving friends. Depression will be discussed in greater detail in the following chapter.

DIVORCE OR FAMILY SEPARATION

Perhaps if adults realized what a teen goes through during a family dissolution, the divorce rate would decrease. In my profession, I see the results every day and am often left with the responsibility of helping to patch lives back together. The emotional trauma experienced by a child or teen because of this crisis is in some ways more devastating than the death of a family member.

Divorce, at its best, is unpleasant for everyone. However, for teenagers it can be the end of hope. Love and security is replaced by anger and resentment. The teen feels out of place, rejected, and alone. He often becomes withdrawn and depressed. Usually, the teenager does not draw a direct connection between his prevailing mood and the divorce. Yet that connection frequently exists.

In one case, a teenager had experienced dropping grades, a change of friends, and been arrested for driving while intoxicated. His father brought him into counseling. I discovered during the first session that the teen's mother had left the family several months earlier. The sessions progressed slowly. Eventually the mother joined in during counseling with the teenager and his father.

Finally, he was able to confront his mother with his true emotions about her leaving. The teen was extremely angry. As he expressed his anger, the healing process began. Over the next few weeks his behavior reversed. Before the end of the year his grades had risen. He began a new relationship with his mother, who unfortunately remained separated from the family but did grow more involved with all her children.

EXCESSIVE FAMILY CONFLICT

My wife of fourteen years and I agree that we married at much too early an age. Yet we married. Conflict, especially during the first year, was intense, painful, and often damaging. However, we stayed married.

Conflict will occur in a family. If the parents can manage it, resolve the conflict openly. If it cannot be managed, the parents need to disagree privately and seek counseling to learn healthy conflict resolution skills.

EXCESSIVE ACADEMIC OR SOCIAL PRESSURE

Our country today has outstanding educational opportunities. Public schools offer curriculum today that challenge what I faced in college. Many of the private schools in our country go even beyond that. I am excited that my children will be able to get an education that will surpass anything I dreamed of years ago.

However, I do not want my children or anyone else's to have unrealistic pressures placed on them. Pressures can come from a variety of sources, as we spoke of earlier. It is not healthy for an adolescent to remain up until 2:00 A.M. incessantly studying to make the dean's list. It is equally unhealthy for boys to become obsessed with building bulk weight for football or losing it for wrestling.

The social pressures to conform, either in dating or other interpersonal relationships, can also lead to stress. There are records of countless incidents of serious depression resulting from friends betraying each other, not being accepted by certain groups, and, in at least one case, being stood up for the senior prom.

Athletics can play an extremely important part in the socialization process. Dating and other friendships are not only normal but necessary to development. However, as parents, we must observe to assure that there is a balance including study, socializing, and other activities. If the pressure becomes excessive, immediate action to reduce the stress must be taken.

PAINFUL LOSS: A BROKEN ROMANCE

The Romeo and Juliet scenario described in chapter 1 is a classic one. It has been the theme for Shakespeare, *West Side Story*, and probably many suicide attempts. When a teen romance ends, view it (depending upon the intensity of the relationship) as being as traumatic as divorce. Probably to the adolescent it is a divorce. A "breakup" can be even more traumatic if it was forced by parents. That is an extremely risky maneuver for parents to become involved in and should be considered in depth. It is at best a gamble, and the stakes are excessive.

MOVING

To an adult, moving can mean a promotion or a new opportunity. However, to an adolescent it can be "the end of the world," as one sixteen-year-old explained to me.

In chapter 2 we discussed the significance of a social network. Second to parents, this social network may be the most important factor in adolescent personality development. Leaving that network behind is threatening and can result in tremendous stress. Obviously, moving can not always be avoided. However, caution is advised when such a possibility is being considered. In fact, whenever possible, moving during late adolescence should be avoided.

Needless to say, children need to be given input into any decision that will affect them as severely as a major relocation.

LACK OF FRIENDS

For whatever reason, occasionally a teen will lack friends. Whether this is a sudden development or one that is chronic, it should concern the parent. As parents we can easily observe whether our teenagers are involved with others. If a teen receives or makes few telephone calls, it may be there is a lack of significant peer relationships.

Dating is one of the primary social activities during adolescence. It is an integral part of the growing up process. Through dating, teenagers can learn a wide variety of communication and social skills and begin to interpret behavior in a more sophisticated way. Often a teen will not be involved in dating. That can lead to discouragement and sometimes even depression, especially among female adolescents. Parental encouragement and possible action is required in support of the teen in such a case. Discouragement of this nature cannot be allowed to evolve into serious depression or a damaged self-concept.

BLENDING FAMILIES

Remarriage of a parent after divorce or death of a spouse can present unusual stress to an adolescent. That is particularly true if the marriage brings new children into the home.

It is interesting that blending families can be as stressful as the divorce that originally separated the family. At the outset it sometimes appears that there are no problems in blending families and, in fact, that it may appear to solve problems. Whereas that may occasionally be true, it is indeed rare. I often recommend families who intend to be joined through remarriage to consult a trained professional as a preventive measure and to ease the transition. This is even more true if adolescents are involved.

EXTENDED VACATION PERIODS

During extended vacation periods (especially summer vacations) some adolescents experience problems. This is especially true with those who have no brothers or sisters or friends. During the school year the adolescent may depend on his teachers and friends for support. Throughout the vacation that support system is gone, and it can become a tremendous problem for the teenager.

FOR FURTHER THOUGHT

1. Make a list of the stresses in your life at the present time. Include items outlined in the chapter and other related or unrelated areas. Include positive stresses, such as promotions, raises, inheritances, and so on.

2. How do you handle excessive stress levels? Do you share your thoughts and feelings with someone? Do you involve yourself in some kind of vigorous activity or sport? Are you able to take breaks and brief or extended vacations? Consider what children are learning from you about how to deal with stress. What do they see you doing with it?

3. List the methods of relaxation you have tried. Note which ones worked and which did not. Consider other possibilities for relaxation.

4. Evaluate the stress levels of significant teenagers in your life. How skilled are they at dealing with those stresses? Do they have a significant person, particularly an adult (other than a parent), whom they can use as a pressure release valve (i.e., someone who will listen unconditionally and caringly)?

5. Think about how teens you know respond to adults. Are their interactions positive or negative? If a teen you know has no significant relationships with a caring adult, decide what you can do to encourage such a relationship. Formalize and write a plan to accomplish that without pushing, forcing, or antagonizing the teenager for whom you are concerned.

The Lord is near to the brokenhearted, and saves those who are crushed in spirit.

—Psalm 34:18

First our pleasures die—and then our hopes, and then our fears, and when these are dead, the debt is due. Dust claims dust, and we die too.

—Percy Bysshe Shelley, *Death*

4

DEPRESSION

THE COMMON COLD

In some cases severe depression can evolve into self-destructive behavior. In fact, one study found depressed teens are 500 times more likely to commit suicide than those who reported no significant symptoms of depression.

Depression is referred to as the "common cold" of emotional problems. Most people report some experience of depression during their lifetimes. For the purposes of this chapter, when the term *depression* is used, it means more than a mere reaction of discouragement or despair. Here more appropriately it will be referred to as a combination of any number of *symptoms* that will be listed later.

DEFINING DEPRESSION

As common as depression is, it is difficult to define. Depending on the source of the definition, it can vary. Some define it as a mood of sadness, despair, and discouragement. Others would call it an attitude of hopelessness and inadequacy accompanied by a lowering level of activity. Yet, other sources would define depression as consisting of negative feelings including painful dejection, difficulty in thinking, and a general slowing of physical and mental activity. Probably an adequate definition would involve some elements of all the above explanations.

It is common to see someone and comment that he "looks depressed." That may be because of the person's drawn face, slow gait, or general appearance of sadness and lethargy. If we see that in adults, we may question them about it in a caring gesture. However, if this is observed in adolescence, there is cause for immediate alarm. Generally, teens hide depression. Some people refer to it as "masking." Sometimes consciously and at other times unconsciously, the despair is disguised. A facade of some sort may replace the true mood of despondency.

DIFFERENCES WITH TEENS

Generally speaking, depression in teenagers is a very slowly evolving process. It is difficult to detect because of its gradual nature and because the symptoms are somewhat different from those in adults.

The origins of adolescent depression are complex. Many events can and do occur which, when combined, can lead to depression. In many modern American families one of the most commonplace origins is the mishandling of anger.

Appropriate expression of anger is one of the keys to avoiding adolescent emotional problems, including depression. We will discuss this phenomenon in great detail later. Briefly, however, forcing a child to withhold or suppress anger can clearly lead to considerable emotional difficulty and eventually lead to depression.

This is complicated even further when parents attempt to take responsibility for adolescents by forcing them to do something they don't want to do. Pressure of that sort can lead to more passive forms of expressing anger that are extremely destructive. Misdirected expression of anger is also described later. It is likewise a part of adolescent depression and one of its frightening aspects.

Most depressed teenagers I deal with are angry. Their underlying anger can take various forms of expression. Many times we find that such maladies as anorexia, self-mutilation, and even suicide are motivated by a deep sense of anger. On more than one occasion suicide has been attempted as a vindictive attempt to "get even." In many of those cases, adolescents have ended their lives to hurt someone else. This is one dramatic kind of acting out. However, it is an extreme and rare case. Most symptoms of adolescent depression are less dramatic and extremely difficult to detect.

RECOGNIZING DEPRESSION

There is no way of knowing precisely what causes depression. It is usually a slowly developing response and occurs over a long period of time. It is complicated with teens because of their lack of accurate reporting of those feelings. An early adolescent will often manifest depression by what some people would call rebellious or immature behavior. That behavior could include temper tantrums, running away, or self-destructive actions such as getting into fights. Behaviors similar to those may, in fact, be a request for help in disguise. Young adolescents, especially boys, are often unwilling or unable to relate their true feelings, so they resort to disruptive behavior, which speaks for them.

DEPRESSION IN EARLY ADOLESCENCE

A friend of mine asked me to work with his eleven-year-old son who was having temper tantrums. I agreed to do so, but only if both parents accompanied the youngster into therapy. During the first session I spent a great deal of time focusing on the child, playing and joking with him to make him more at ease. I brought him a doughnut and then an orange soda while his father, a young dentist, watched in horror.

Actually, I knew the child didn't eat like that at home, and although I don't recommend that sort of food regularly, it did help me to gain rapport. We talked about TV, movies, and soccer until the youngster was speaking freely. Not once had I addressed the parents or even asked them why the family was visiting me.

I suddenly turned to the child and asked, "By the way, do you get to spend enough time with your mom"?

"Sure—I guess," he answered. "I see her all the time."

"OK. How about your dad?" I already knew the answer. The child looked at his father as if expecting him to answer. I encouraged him to respond. Then the young dentist nodded his head as if giving permission.

"No, I don't get enough time with him. I never see him except at breakfast and on weekends once in a while."

"Now, that is not true," his mother spoke up. "You ride to school with him two days a week."

"Yeah, but he is always in too much of a hurry to talk. Besides, he's grouchy in the morning."

"Well—" The mother began to speak, but I interrupted.

"OK. We'll have to see what we can do. We're here to find an answer to a situation, not figure out blame. And certainly nobody is being accused. Tom, just for the record, how much time do you guess you spend with Kevin in a day, excluding meals, TV, and driving in the car?"

As I stated earlier, Tom is a friend of mine. He knew that I seldom asked such a question without knowing the answer ahead of time. Yet he cooperated, which is commendable.

After pausing he finally replied, "If you take those away, the answer is probably none, as you already knew."

"Now, how many tantrums is Kevin having in a day?" I directed the question to nobody in particular. Finally, his mother, Sheila, spoke.

"Probably three or four including school and home combined. That is just a rough estimate. Maybe more or less on any given day."

We decided to graph the results of my prescribed treatment. Tom began by spending one minute per day and adding one minute a day with Kevin until he reached fourteen minutes per day. This time was to be spent intensely on a one-on-one basis. No TV, books, cars, or meals were allowed. I suggested they wrestle, chase each other, play tag, or ride around the neighborhood piggyback. If they chose to wrestle, Kevin would get to win six days per week. I wanted the attention to be palpable, visceral, and physical. Basically, it was a literal "hands on" approach. This case is a dramatic example of what intense attention can do.

Ten days later the tantrums disappeared. As quality

time with dad increased, the tantrums proportionally decreased. Another way of stating the result is that it only took ten minutes of intense personal attention per day to satisfy this young adolescent. We had one visit together in the office and one on the phone. The child has not had a tantrum in over three years and certainly is no longer depressed.

In many ways Kevin's behavior was a direct signal to his parents that he needed more time. Perhaps his tantrum was a way of asking Dad to give more attention. Had that situation continued, there would probably have been serious consequences.

ACTING OUT DEPRESSION

In later adolescence, depression comes to take on more classical symptoms, but is still difficult to detect. The teenager may describe a sense of overwhelming boredom, lack of concentration, lack of energy, or a general report of lethargy and isolation.

Some of those symptoms are admittedly expressed by all teens. However, if we observe them in combination with some of the other symptoms listed in this chapter, we certainly need to take notice.

These symptoms can be accompanied by a similar acting out episode as demonstrated earlier. If it is exhibited as being of a sexual or aggressive nature, it should be responded to seriously.

Acting out may be the human "fail-safe mechanism." I like to think that God installed survival systems in His creatures. With adolescents I see this system as the acting out phenomenon. Perhaps we are not perceptive enough to observe adolescent depression in early stages. Whereas it is difficult to detect in the early stages, it is almost impossible to ignore it when the teen is acting out. However, we seldom recognize the behavior for what it really is. To define it more clearly, the acting out is a way of screaming to the adult—"Help me!"

A CASE OF ACTING OUT DEPRESSION

Tonya was a beautiful sixteen-year-old girl. By the time she arrived at my office her family had survived outrageous acting out behavior on her part. That ultimately led to her second suicide attempt, which failed, thanks to competent paramedics and a highly trained emergency room hospital staff. It was certainly questionable at the time whether or not she would survive.

Her parents brought her into counseling only after a particular kind of acting out. Unbelievably, the suicide attempts did not cause them to seek a counselor.

Tonya had become involved with a new boyfriend, who was causing everybody trouble. He was a twenty-year-old high school dropout and really an adolescent himself. He had persuaded Tonya to sneak out of her bedroom to be with him on various occasions. She was finally apprehended by her parents. While under the influence of drugs and still high, she confessed that she and her new boyfriend were sexually involved.

Because of the history of suicide attempts, I suggested hospitalization to the family. The parents refused but agreed to a psychiatric and psychological evaluation. Both evaluations found her to be depressed but suggested out-patient counseling could be attempted as long as she was supervised closely by her parents. The family agreed to see me twice a week initially.

On a subsequent visit, Tonya admitted to continually sneaking out after she had been caught again by her parents. During that session I began to chastise her in front of her mother and father. They thought I was going to scold her for sneaking out.

"Tonya, it is obvious to me that you are having problems. I mean, let's face it. You are nearly seventeen years old, and you can't even sneak out of your bedroom without getting caught. You obviously are lacking in some very important skills." I turned to her father.

"Mr. Jones, you really have a problem here. It is apparent to me that someone has failed as a parent. Let's be serious. You've got a teenager here who can't even sneak out!" He stared silently, almost as if unable to speak.

"Your daughter needs more direction. I'll tell you what I want to happen. I would like for you to get up each morning for the next two weeks at 2:00 A.M. and give Tonya lessons on how to sneak out of her bedroom window without getting caught. The lessons will last between fifteen and thirty minutes. What do you think, should they be more like fifteen or closer to thirty?"

He had no immediate response. I assume he was trying to figure out what I had directed him to do.

"Yes," I continued, "I know it's a difficult decision, but which do you think would be better, fifteen or thirty minutes daily? Probably you are a good teacher, but Tonya might be a slow learner."

By making the length of the sessions an issue of debate, it was presumed he would follow through on the task. That effectively reduced his resistance at doing what I had suggested.

"I guess fifteen to twenty minutes," he finally conceded. That was done above the protests of his daughter.

"Great. I agree. Both of you should be able to handle this in that time period."

I ended the session with no further discussion. I had based my action on certain assumptions. Mr. Jones was an optometrist. I knew he worked long hours and had little time to spend with his daughter. She obviously wanted male attention but would not have agreed to go out socially with her father because of her anger toward him. Mr. Jones was extremely religious, and I assumed he would be compliant because he was referred to me by his priest. To cover myself, I called his priest and explained what I was trying to accomplish. He agreed to cooperate. Less than an hour later he called me back and said Mr. Jones had contacted him to discuss the assignment. The priest encouraged Mr. Jones to cooperate, and he did so.

The result was rather predictable. It is no fun to sneak out of your bedroom window if you have a parent supervising you on how to do a better job of it. Tonya and her father were also assured of fifteen to twenty minutes of interaction daily, which in this case was something she needed. In addition, she was so sleepy after three or four days of lessons she lost interest in seeing her boyfriend at 3:00 A.M.

After eight lessons in a row, Mr. Jones and Tonya agreed that to continue was insane and decided that their priest and I were in cahoots. They figured that they would "show us" and agreed to spend their time together each day playing tennis at a more convenient hour.

When they returned to counseling, the family was much happier, and Tonya's acting out had disappeared. Her depression soon improved, and she became very active in school. She went on to graduate from high school and was later homecoming queen at the college she attended. Today she is happily married, the mother of a toddler, and active in her church and community.

THE IMPORTANCE OF TIME

A recent study found that the average American parent spends very little time in one-on-one interaction with his children. In fact, a Penn State University study found that on an average, adults spend less than seven minutes per week in intense personal time with their children. To be fair, they excluded television, meals, and commuting time.

Nevertheless, if that is true (and my professional experience indicates it is), we face a tragedy of enormous proportion. It demonstrates a lack of leadership in the American home and is a national disgrace. Perhaps some cases of depression, suicide, and certainly divorce are reflections of that statistic.

In one study it was found that most teens who commit suicide come from depressed backgrounds. In fact, depression in parents was found to be possibly a stronger predictor of suicide than a history of previous attempts by the teenager. Another study found suicidal children showed greater depressive symptoms including running away and "sneaking out" than nonsuicide-prone children. During therapy those children expressed profound feelings of abandonment. The majority were either physically abused or simply ignored.

In both of the case examples above, time was the missing ingredient. With increased time and attention from the parents, the problem behavior and depression decreased. If the depression had continued unchecked for a more extended period of time, complex biochemical changes could have occurred. Then the depression could have taken on an endogenous nature.

EXOGENOUS AND ENDOGENOUS DEPRESSION

Many professionals refer to depression as having origins of an exogenous or endogenous nature. In fact, depression can have exogenous origins and later develop an endogenous nature. Exogenous sources of depression are those that have an external or social connection. Any of the events listed in the chapter on adolescent stress, such as a broken romance or moving to a new location, can become sources of exogenous depression.

Endogenous depression is usually the result of complex biochemical changes within the body. In those cases, or in any case of prolonged depression, it is vital for a psychiatrist or other medical doctor to be consulted. Extended periods of severe depression can lead to a loss of contact with reality, which is extremely dangerous and possibly life-threatening. Severe depression must be dealt with by highly trained professionals. Certainly, if there is any question as to the severity of the depression, consultation with a psychiatrist or other medical doctor is advised.

GUILT AND FEAR

Guilt and fear are also contributing factors to depression. Some adults may find themselves using these as a means of disciplining or motivating teenagers. In a few select cases it may be warranted. In fact, the desired short term result may occur. However, unwarranted or excessive use of either can be extremely damaging.

There are obvious situations of danger when it is appropriate to use fear. Shouting to a child playing in the street when a car is approaching may cause fear. Yet it may also save that child's life. This is one obvious example of using fear motivation appropriately. There are fewer instances in which guilt can be wisely used as a measure of discipline. To make a generalization, it is best avoided.

CONCLUSION

Adolescent depression occurs in predictable stages and is easily masked. It sometimes is manifested by a combination of the following:

EARLY STAGES

Inability to concentrate
Excessive daydreaming
Withdrawal from friends
Impulsive acts (seemingly without forethought)
Decreasing grades
Change in eating or sleeping habits

MIDDLE STAGES

Acts of aggression
Rapid mood swings
Loss of interest in work, school, etc.
Loss of friends
Boredom
Preoccupation with physical complaints—headaches,
    stomachaches, etc.
Mild rebelliousness
Sudden changes in personality

DANGER STAGE

Appearing visibly depressed
Anorexia
Alcohol or drug abuse
Suicide threats, attempts, or gestures
Giving away prized possessions
Preoccupation with death
Expressions of helplessness
Loss of values
Extreme aggressive behavior
Overt extreme rebelliousness

FOR FURTHER THOUGHT

1. Post a list of the signs and symptoms of teenage depression for quick and frequent reference.

2. Recall your own adolescence. What events or situations triggered your depression? Looking back, were they significant or trivial? At that time, what were your perceptions of those events or situations?

3. Tune your awareness to a teenager with whom you are acquainted. Mentally note if any signs or symptoms fit. If you can answer "yes" to three or more symptoms, consider talking with the teenager openly. Also consider talking with teachers and friends concerning their observations. Think of other teenagers you come in contact with. Do any of them show signs of depression?

4. Consider how you would discipline a teen. Compare these methods with those you would use with a toddler or young child. How are they different? How are they the same? Are the consequences of behavior appropriate?

5. How do your methods of discipline compare with those you received as a young child and teen?

6. How much quality time do you spend with adolescents? With other significant relationships? Do you want to do anything to change it?

And so, as those who have been chosen of God, holy and beloved, put on a heart of compassion, kindness, humility, gentleness and patience; bearing with one another, and forgiving each other whoever has a complaint against anyone; just as the Lord forgave you, so also should you. And beyond all these things put on love, which is the perfect bond of unity.

—Colossians 3:12–14

History teaches us that there is no substitute for the family, if we are to have a society that stands for human beings at their best.

—Ray Lyman Wilbur

5

FAMILY DYNAMICS

SCAPEGOAT

David's parents argued on a regular basis. When he was five years old, his father returned home from work late one evening and participated in an intense disagreement with David's mother. During the argument both made threats and screamed loudly. David didn't understand all that was being said or even what the disagreement was about.

Yet he was intensely frightened when the threats began. They shouted something about leaving and then something else about killing each other. In his mind these were not words but reality. David fearfully began to back out of the living room. As he did, he stumbled into the coffee table and knocked over an expensive lamp, which crashed to the floor.

David's parents rushed over and began scolding him for breaking the lamp. After a few minutes they stopped complaining and helped David clean up the broken glass. Mother then retired to the kitchen and father into his bedroom. Within thirty minutes they were speaking to each other as if nothing had happened.

At that very moment, on some level of consciousness, David began to think of himself almost as a magician. It may not have been on a level of acute awareness, but learning took place. He began to think, "They may yell at me, but at least nobody is going to get killed. I have the power to make them stop yelling at each other."

Three weeks later a similar problem occurred between David's parents. The yelling and threats soon followed. Perhaps unconsciously and perhaps not, David knocked over a pot of boiling soup. Some of it landed on his ankle and burned him severely. His parents responded with a combination of fear, pity, and anger. Nevertheless, they didn't argue with each other any longer that night. David's learning was reinforced.

Several months later David turned over an aquarium. Later he cut his hand when he "mistakenly" put it through a window. His parents began to use various terms when referring to David. He was "accident prone, a problem child, clumsy."

In the second grade he was beaten up on three different occasions by older boys. Later that year he was caught stealing money from his teacher's purse. Time and time again the parents were brought closer together by constantly worrying and wondering what was going to happen next. In the fifth grade he was caught shoplifting. At age fifteen he was arrested for burglarizing a house. The entire family had to go to court on that occasion.

Shortly before his eighteenth birthday, David was apprehended for robbing a convenience market. On the eve of that birthday and before his court appearance, David ended his life. He left behind a note to his parents and claimed, "I died for your sins." The family doctor claimed David had obviously been psychotic when he wrote the note.

Perhaps. Or just maybe, in David's mind, he was subconsciously caught in a trap from which he was unable to escape. He certainly appeared to save his parent's marriage, at least in his mind. Many people would refer to David as the scapegoat. He was the person who assumed the family's pathology, or the family's problems. David seemed to see himself as the savior of the family. And in many ways it appears he may have sacrificed his own well-being for the purpose of keeping his parents together. Or perhaps that's just esoteric philosophy.

Nevertheless, within three months of his death, David's parents divorced.

The process David entered is not one completely understood. The relationships involved unconscious as well as conscious messages somehow sent and received. It is also not easy to affix responsibility in those cases. No one can actually say who was responsible for the role David played in the family. To attempt assigning exclusive responsibility would be missing the point.

Those decisions are agreed on corporately on an unspoken level. David and his parents shared in the decision making. The only time anyone broke the rules was when David left his suicide note. It ended the game.

IMPORTANCE OF FAMILY RELATIONSHIPS

Various studies have found that one of the major characteristics of those adolescents who attempt suicide is an absence of meaningful relationships with significant adults. I have interviewed many teenagers after they attempted suicide. Most claim they can remember no adult to whom they ever felt close. Others will claim they once felt warmth, but it was toward the absent parent.

The importance of intimate relationships cannot be overstated. Psychologists have found an assortment of characteristics to be significant of young adolescent males who would attempt suicide. The primary one is the lack of an effective father figure in the home. If the father lives with the family, he is likely to be extremely successful and heavily involved in his work. One study investigated attempts of suicide by males who had attended boarding schools. One implication is they were seriously affected by being separated from influential parent relationships. Death, divorce, and strained relationships with the mother figure have also proved to be significant factors.

Girls who attempt suicide are likely to come from a home where the mother is a domineering and narcissistic figure, who is preoccupied with herself. The father in those cases is likely to be weak and ineffectual. The adolescent female is then likely to turn to her boyfriend or his family for support. If they are unable to replace the parental figures, the young lady usually experiences depressive episodes. She may become pregnant, or think she is. It is interesting that she is also apt to be a heavy smoker (which is also true of suicide-prone adolescent boys).

LEARNING DEPRESSION AND SUICIDE

We learn from our parents how to deal with emotions. Depressed and suicidal youngsters are likely to come from depressed and suicide-prone families. It is perhaps unfair, but mothers certainly have a greater impact in this respect than do fathers. In fact, one study indicated chronic depression in the mother was one of the most reliable predicters of suicide proneness in teenagers.

Violence can also be learned or modeled from significant adults. More than 80 percent of all adolescent suicide attempters have a history of physical or corporal punishment in their family. That appears to be more true with adolescent males than females.

It has been proved repeatedly that child abusers were abused as children. This is true in the case of both sexual and physical abuse. Violence in any form, even if intended positively, will result in more violence. It may be directed toward others, or it may be directed inwardly in the form of depression or ultimately suicide. The learning will be effective.

This certainly indicates that parents should strongly consider avoiding the use of frequent physical discipline with their children. Corporal punishment is indeed a risk, and it appears that the odds may be against the parent who uses it.

There is also a more philosophical area of consideration. We need to investigate the question of the nature of children.

NATURE/NURTURE

Medieval Christians, and later the pilgrims who fled to this country seeking religious freedom, had a philosophy that was somewhat critical of children. In the opinion of

authorities of that era, children were to be harshly controlled. Their reasoning was that children were possessed
by demons. Following that logic, parents were given de-
facto permission and sanction to apply harsh disciplinary
measures to their children. After all, they rationalized,
"We are doing the children a favor." There are many
records of those who proceeded to beat the demons out of
their children.

That philosophy still pervades in many homes today.
Even more alarming is the popularity of some "experts"
who continue to espouse such a philosophy. One popular
radio commentator recently referred to children as "uncivilized and depraved." I literally shuddered, thinking of the
thousands of people influenced by that approach. I see the
results of such a point of view in my office daily.

I am not a radio commentator. I am also not a researcher or theoretician. I am a psychotherapist. I apply
certain principles I have learned through the years. I visit
daily with people who are having difficulty. I have not
kept records, but a reasonable estimate would be that I
have seen several thousand families in my professional
career. I have yet to see one family in which that philosophy had a good result.

I can also say that "beating the demons" out of children
is not only ineffective but harmful and possibly abusive.
There is no basis to support the philosophy that beatings
are productive. It is exceptionally dangerous and could
indeed lead to depression, self-destructiveness, and ultimately suicide.

Such a point of view also ignores the positive effect of
nurture. Adolescents who are exposed to parental warmth
and love will probably have a more successful life in all
aspects than those who receive the opposite.

There is overwhelming research available that indicates
relationships with nurturing parents provide the teenager
with personality strength and depth. This depth enables
the adolescent to cope with stress presented by the hurried
society refered to earlier. Nurture (classically defined as
environmental influence) can have a positive effect on
teenagers.

The nature/nuture issue is a significant one because it

reflects our core value about childrearing. If we view adolescents as merely uncivilized and depraved, their behavior
will likely reflect that point of view. However, if we regard
them as positive potential, or what good they could become,
then their behavior will be more positive. Resigning ourselves to the point that teens cannot be influenced by
nurture may even be inconsistent with biblical example.

CHRIST'S VIEW OF THE NATURE OF CHILDREN

It appears paradoxical that medieval Christians approached the nature issue as they did. These religious
forefathers seemed to ignore Christ's example in many
ways. The Bible provides examples of Jesus Christ nurturing babies and children (Luke 18:15–17). When the disciples tried to prevent youngsters from touching Jesus, He
rebuked them and took the children on His lap (Mark
10:14–16). On two occasions He raised children from the
dead (Luke 7:11–17; Mark 5:22–24, 35–43). His compassion and kindness went so far as to gently remind Jairus to
feed his daughter. Jesus realized that in the parents' joy
over her restoration to life, they might overlook her state
of hunger.

Jesus demonstrated a view of people that exhibited love,
forgiveness, and was filled with positive expectancy. Examples include: the woman at the well (John 4:6–14); the
leper (Mark 1:40–42); the woman hemorrhaging (Mark
5:25–34); the woman caught in adultery (John 8:3–11);
and the thief on the cross (Luke 23:42, 43). None of those
examples indicate that Christ had a negative point of view
of children or adults. He appeared to expect the best from
people, and His positive expectations reaped positive results. This was true even though some examples were from
people with less than flawless characters.

His example simply did not reflect the point of view that
children need to be beaten. Rather, His love, compassion,
and tenderness were far more powerful in their influence.

HOMEOSTASIS

One dictionary defines *homeostasis* as "the maintenance
of steady states . . . (in the organism)." Family therapists

share a similar meaning of the term, implying that a family, similar to the body and the environment, seeks to maintain balance.

If we visualize a mobile, perhaps the picture will be clearer. The mobile is in a delicate state of balance that keeps it moving. If one part of the mobile is damaged or somehow bent out of proportion, the rest of the mobile will compensate and form a new balance, albeit an awkward one.

Many family therapists have come to view the family as an organism that functions in a way similar to the mobile. At various times this is demonstrated during counseling sessions. As one family member becomes more functional, another may become less. The balance is maintained.

One case demonstrated this dramatically.

*AN ILLUSTRATION OF HOMEOSTASIS

The Brown family illustrates well the concept of family homeostasis. Tom was the forty-two-year-old father, and Jane was the forty-three-year-old mother. The children included Jan, a fifteen-year-old girl; Brad, twelve; and Bill, ten.

In most ways the family was from a typical middle-class background. They were very involved in the community and with their children. Tom had a high-paying job with a secure company. He was well-liked as were his children. Jane worked as a physician's secretary and was successful in her occupation. The entire family was very active in their church.

The primary complaint for this family was Jane's addiction to various prescription drugs. On one occasion Tom brought a fifty-gallon plastic trash bag filled with various prescription drugs and dumped it on my office floor. He had found them hidden throughout the home, and many of them were not even opened. Most of the medications were free samples Jane had stolen from her office.

Jane had been using the drugs for quite a few years, and much of the time was almost helplessly intoxicated. The problem had mushroomed to the point that, two years before, her daughter, Jan, had effectively taken over maternal responsibilities and performed them meticulously. The family had developed a balance, revolving around the daughter's maternal skills and the mother's ineffectiveness. Actually, it worked out quite well.

Problems occurred only periodically when Jane would start getting better and try to resume her responsibilities. Unfortunately, she was not as efficient as her daughter, and that consistently led to disruptions. Eventually, as a result of her anxiety and disappointment, Jane would return to her drugs and once again remove herself psychologically from the "mother" role. Jan would resume the role, and the family resumed a more functional balance.

The therapeutic challenge became to let Jane recover from addiction and to let Jan return to the daughter's role (which she longed to do) without creating undue disruption. Basically, we had to build a new balance. It was accomplished over a period of months. Eventually Jane quit her job and entered drug rehabilitation. She began a slow recovery process that involved a renewal of her faith in God. In fact, it was that faith and the strength she received from the promises of God's Word that enabled her to recover.

Today she has successfully reentered her family and occupies her time counseling with other women who have drug problems. Her daughter is a college student and has resumed a healthy relationship with her mother.

Unfortunately, as illustrated above, sometimes homeostasis means a balance of imbalance. The balance is often dysfunctional, in spite of the condition of balance. In those cases the family has adapted to a pathological or unhealthy norm. This is actually more common than one would probably expect.

HAROLD

Harold was a successful architect and had reached that success at an unusually early age. Over the past thirteen months, however, his life had deteriorated. At twenty-eight years of age, he lived with his parents, was unmarried, and was experiencing severe depression. He had been admitted to a psychiatric hospital and then left against his physician's advice after a few days.

Later he came to my office accompanied by his parents. He was openly discussing suicide at this point but refused further psychiatric hospitalization. His parents likewise refused to encourage him to return to the hospital. Assisted by psychiatric consultation I agreed to see him in therapy but only on specific terms. He agreed to no suicide attempts, and we were to visit with each other three times per week initially. His parents agreed to supervise him closely at home over the next few weeks and to assure that he attended therapy and completed all tasks assigned to him.

Among other things, I required that he jog daily with a friend while discussing future goals. A psychiatrist administered antidepressant medication. I kept him busy ten to twelve hours per day with therapeutic tasks and assignments. He was not allowed to listen to any music or watch any television without prior approval. He was required to read certain books and listen to certain cassette tapes and report on them. He was not allowed to read the newspaper or listen to news broadcasts. His food consumption was also prescribed as well as a vitamin regimen.

During the third week of treatment he grew extremely emotional when discussing his family. We were scheduled for a family therapy session two days later, and we both decided it would be better to discuss family material at that time. A breakthrough of a small nature followed.

Harold confronted his parents at the next session with an issue that had haunted him since his high school days. However, he had not previously discussed it. Basically, during a family argument he had been told, "When you get your life together, we are going to get divorced." He asked them (appropriately) how he could ever get better if it meant that he would be responsible for his parents' divorce.

Harold had allowed his behavior to be controlled by that fear for more than twelve years. Actually, his parents had a relatively stable marriage. Harold's perception of reality was distorted. Nevertheless, he based his behavior on that perception, and, consequently, his behavior was somewhat distorted.

Harold was no different than any of us. We all base our

behavior on the way we perceive reality. What reality truly is becomes irrelevant as far as behavioral response is concerned. Each individual's perception is going to be somewhat different, neurologically as well as socially. To tell someone you "see things differently" is always going to be true. Harold saw things differently. As a result, he almost destroyed his life.

In the weeks that followed, Harold's family joined him in counseling. His attitude and behavior improved markedly. Within three months he decided to move to another city. Two years and two weeks after I first met Harold, he was married. Today, he is still married, has two children, and is leading a happy life.

And his parents are still together.

FAMILY AS A SYSTEM

The family is not the origin of all adolescent problems. It can, however, be the beginning of an *answer* to some of the difficulties teenagers experience. On many occasions I have been approached by families who requested that I work with their teenagers. In virtually all cases I eventually end up seeing the entire family in counseling. In more than half of those cases after diagnostic interviews I recommended marriage counseling.

One of my professors once said that he had never seen a problem child and seldom seen a child who had a problem. In his experience, the difficulties he dealt with were family problems rather than child problems. One famous psychotherapist simply refuses to see individuals in counseling sessions at all. Another refuses to see fragments of families. There are dozens of stories of a partial family (without all the members present) being refused treatment by the latter psychotherapist until they can return with the family intact. One authority in the field of family counseling has been quoted as claiming, "There's no such thing as an individual. An individual is only an artifact of a family system."

The family system's perspective views all behavior as a function of family relationships. In some cases, such as Harold's, behavior is much more logical when understood in that way. In his case, the family was required to be treated together for Harold to progress individually.

FAMILY CONFLICT RESOLUTION

Early adolescents and even some late teens still think in concrete terms, yet are developing some capacity for abstract reasoning. Because of the frustration of that dissonance, a teen may tend to overreact to disagreement at any level. If conflict is left unresolved for an extended period of time, it can develop to create major problems.

All of us, as parents or adult friends of children, will occasionally "blow it." We will indeed make mistakes. At those times it is important to be able to admit the mistake to the child and apologize. On other occasions our adolescents will merely perceive reality somewhat differently than we do. At those times, empathic and noncritical conversation must occur. A sharing of separate realities will usually calm the disagreement. Minds may remain unchanged. However, emotions and perceptions will be clarified.

In any case it is best to attempt resolving unfinished business with teenagers. Anything left unclarified can lead to resentment and hostility, which can only create further conflicts.

FOR FURTHER THOUGHT

1. Think about your family of origin (i.e., you, any siblings, and your parents or guardians). What form of discipline was used in your home? Were all persons treated equally and fairly? Were children encouraged to express themselves? How did it effect you?

2. As you recall answers to the above questions, notice what emotions you are experiencing. Are they sad, angry, joyful, or fearful? Are you comfortable with those feelings?

3. Write down anything you wish you had said as a child or teen to a parent or guardian. If the person is still living, consider what it would be like to say it. Does it still need to be said? If the person is not living, can you say it out loud?

4. Consider the patterns of interaction in your nuclear family (i.e., you, a spouse, and your own children). Are there similarities to those of your family of origin? What differences do you note? Are you satisfied with those patterns? Are there any changes you would like to make?

5. Does your family have any kind of forums, meetings, or discussion groups? Do teens and children have speaking and or voting rights on decisions made for the family? How are individual responsibilities and expectations determined as children and teens grow and mature?

Fathers, do not provoke your children to anger; but bring them up in the discipline and instruction of the Lord.

—Ephesians 6:4

How poor are they that have no patience! What wound did ever heal but by degrees?

—Shakespeare—Othello, Ac. II Sc. 3

6

CHALLENGES OF LATE ADOLESCENCE

EYE OF THE STORM

If adolescence is a stormy period, late adolescence is the eye of the storm. Late adolescence usually occurs between ages 16 and 20. It is normal for special challenges to occur during this period. Surprisingly that is even more true if there has been little difficulty prior to this age.

The term *challenge* may be somewhat reactionary. Actually, it is more of a developmental stage. In some cases, the stage can become a crisis as a result of the family's response. It is fairly common during this stage for an adolescent to test limits. The patience and love of parents can be tested as never before.

FRUSTRATION AND ANGER

An emotional state often noticed during late adolescence is characterized by excessive frustration. The teen's drive for independence is at an apex by this age. Nevertheless, multiple obstacles to independence are confronted. When a teenager continually finds his independence blocked, he can become unconsciously frustrated and consequently hostile.

This is simple to understand when considered from a life-span perspective. Basically, the late adolescent is on the verge of adulthood. The freedom and independence perceived by teens is quite appealing. They often have many of the traits that accompany maturity. Their entire life up to this point has been in preparation for this new independence. Nevertheless, they continually experience themselves as unable to reach adulthood. The obstacle preventing that step can be perceived as parents, financial resources, or any number of other obstacles. The result of this perceived obstacle can often be frustration.

Thwarted independence adds fuel to the fire of burning dissonance within teenagers. Hundreds of adolescents have ultimately confided in me of their fears and self-doubt about making it on their own. Naturally, most teens do not want to discuss these fears with their parents. When approached or questioned, the defensiveness projected by the teenager is often seen in anger.

Anger frequently builds over a period of years. Teenagers often store it away rather than dealing with it. Eventually, when the adolescent reaches his threshold for suppression of anger, outbursts occur. The focus of the outbursts will usually become parents or other authority figures.

This anger can be released either directly or in some other way. If expression of hostility is not allowed by parents, the anger can occur in more indirect and passive methods. Such methods are actually more destructive than open expression. Unfortunately, this indirectness can a part of one's personality. It is most often noticed during late adolescence. The strength of it may depend on the parents' response.

EMOTIONAL EXPRESSION

It is much better at any age to encourage children to express rather than suppress their emotions. They key is to teach children how to work productively through negative emotions. Well-meaning parents often make the mistake of not allowing children to express negative emotions. Yet we can all admit that it is normal to experience such emotions such as frustration, anxiety, and anger.

Forcing children to deny their feelings is equivalent to forcing them to deny their reality. Denial can only lead to complications. Unfortunately, in my personal and professional experience, the taboo against expression of anger is especially true in homes with religious backgrounds. We often appear to struggle under the myth that it is not acceptable for children to become upset. We may actually condemn the teenager who becomes upset. Actually, anger is a normal response to frustration or fear. The important factor is how we deal with it. It is not healthy at all to constantly repress anger.

Incredibly, I have heard teachers in both Sunday school and junior high school classrooms commenting that "God doesn't love you when you get mad." The implication of that comment is that the angry one is not acting Christlike. I have heard other well-meaning adults imply that if the teenager's life were in harmony with Scriptures there would not be any anger.

The facts remain that we all experience anger. Yet, we require acceptance from God as well as man. A teenager led to believe he is not normal may experience overwhelming confusion, embarrassment, or humiliation and attempt to further squelch the anger by pretending it does not exist. The results can be devastating. As discussed earlier, suppressed anger must eventually be expressed or discharged in some way from the body. If open expression is neither allowed nor learned, the development of indirect but destructive expressions of anger occurs.

INDIRECT EXPRESSIONS OF ANGER

Indirect expressions of anger are most often detected in late adolescence and are the behavioral equivalent of guerrilla warfare. One of the basic tenents of this unconventional style of fighting is "if the enemy outnumbers you, then outfox them." Our country learned in Vietnam that simply outnumbering the foe, and even combining those numbers with superior technology and superior logistics, will not suffice. Others have also learned their lesson.

In Cuba during the early 1960s, Che Guevera and Fidel Castro understood that and successfully overthrew the gov-

ernment of that time, the Batista regime. They realized
victory could not be theirs conventionally. So they conducted small campaigns at which they could not only succeed but also effectively demoralize the enemy. Guevera is
credited with designing the "shotgun minuet." This was a
scenario by which three soldiers strategically placed on
either side of a trail could easily control hundreds of government soldiers. That strategy had the effect of not only
taking the enemy's lives but also of intimidating some
government soldiers to the point that they refused to enter
the jungles.

Misdirected expressions of anger follow the same pattern. Basically, the teenager sees himself in an oppositional
relationship to the parents and other authority sources.
That may be later generalized to all sources of authority.
The teen has seldom been successful at confronting parents directly. Occasionally that is because of the parents'
lack of willingness to allow the child to openly discuss
issues, much less disagree or express any level of frustration.

At some level of consciousness, the late teen then de-
cides to do small things, usually behind the parents' back,
to get even. Those responses are often extremely destructive both to the teenager and to the parents. In fact,
suicide can be an indirect expression of anger to get even
with a parent or some other authority figure.

This can be manifested in various ways. Most often it is
seen in such forms as falling grades, clothing and fashion,
tardiness, eating habits, missing appointments, and so on.
Usually the adolescent will choose avenues that he is certain will be most objectionable to the parents or other
authority figure.

The most frightening aspect is that it can become a part
of a teenager's core personality and accompany him into
adulthood. The behavior is then manifested toward other
authority figures in an unconscious attempt to continue
getting even with the parents. It is as if the person trans-
fers his anger from the parent figure to other authority
figures. That can include a spouse, employer, or supervi-
sor. Obviously, this results in an extremely unhappy and
unsuccessful adult life. It has certainly resulted in a large

number of people being fired from their jobs and has caused many divorces.

It has been stated that all teenagers misdirect their anger to some degree. It has also been suggested that this sort of behavior is more prevelant in conservative populations, even among adults. The potential for its development is primarily dependent on how parents and others respond to overtly expressed anger. If open expression of anger is allowed, there will be no reason for the late teenager to express it discreetly.

THE BROWN FAMILY

On the surface the Brown family was probably everything we would all want in a family. They were extremely cordial, attractive, and financially secure. Mr. Brown was an elder in a large church. His business was successful and nationally known. His father had built the business to a point that it would survive over many generations. Mr. Brown was able to step in, take over, and watch the business grow. Mrs. Brown was a beautiful wife and mother. She had her own business as well, which she enjoyed and from which she received a great deal of gratification.

Their children had all been high achievers and active in school. The two oldest boys were in college. One was in graduate school and had received a full merit scholarship. The eldest daughter was married and had recently returned to the family's hometown with her husband. He entered the family business at the invitation of her father. Their youngest daughter until recently had been "the best and brightest" of the family. She had effortlessly sailed through her junior year in high school. With minimal studying she had never earned any grade below a B.

That had changed.

The last report card reflected all Ds and Fs.

In my office her father expressed the confusion and anger with which they all viewed the situation. He began by very calmly describing the family. Then he came to his youngest daughter's grades. The longer he spoke, the more emotional he became. The more emotional he grew, the more satisfaction his daughter seemed to reflect. Within minutes, he was screaming and waving his arms. At times he even left his chair as he grew more animated. And with the increasing volume, his daughter seemed to appear more and more smug. Within minutes the scenario pieced itself together.

She was very angry at her father. There was little else she could do to get even. He was actually a good parent and did spend time with her. However, he had never allowed her to openly disagree. She had repressed her dissatisfaction for many years. Now her anger was surfacing, but indirectly. The adolescent actually was controlling her father while doing precisely what she wanted. She gained satisfaction from watching him get upset. Somehow, she knew that was the best way to get even.

Several things eventually occurred in this family. Over a period of time in family counseling, the father began to allow his daughter to openly disagree and express certain resentments she had been harboring. The daughter began to realize what she had done by lowering her grades. The immediate response, however, was most interesting.

I directed the parents to completely avoid commenting on her grades. Instead, at the point they felt an urgency to complain about homework or any other academic subject, they were to tell their daughter to go clean up her room. The mother objected that her daughter's room was immaculate. I assured her that it would not remain that way.

Indeed.

Within several months the daughter was once again bringing home As. However, her room had become a disaster. Other family members refused to even enter her room. The daughter loved it. Her final report card reflected all As. She went on to complete high school and graduated from college two and one-half years later. Today she is attending medical school in California and plans to enter a residency program in psychiatry.

RESPONSES TO MISDIRECTED ANGER

Misdirected anger presents a special challenge to parents. Responding to the behavior rewards the teenager and, in fact, strengthens the likelihood the behavior will be repeated. Basically, the teenager is looking for a response. In the example given above, Mr. Brown was doing exactly what daughter wanted. The goal of her behavior was to make her father angry.

The only way to weaken daughter's response was to ignore it. Because that was nearly impossible to do, the parents were given something to complain about. Asking them to avoid responding at all could have led them to becoming indirect. A dirty bedroom is one of the least harmful of alternatives for expressing anger. Therefore, the parents were directed to focus their attention on it.

The daughter quickly realized that if her grades remained low she would not be accepted into college. The "pay-off" for her bad grades was removed when father began to ignore them. Since, in her case, making good grades required little effort, her grades naturally increased. Paralleling the increase in grades was a proportional deterioration in the appearance of her bedroom. Her father was directed to act frustrated and upset about the messy room, but in reality he didn't care. However, the more he complained, the messier the room became. And her grades continued to rise.

Within time, the daughter realized what was occurring, yet she continued to "cooperate" with her father. Now as a young adult, when she returns home for a visit, she is always very careful to leave her bedroom in a mess. And her father is always very careful to complain. They laugh. It seems to work.

LEAVING HOME

A large number of teenagers I see in late adolescence are struggling with the issue of leaving home. It is a traumatic period for them and parents alike. That seems to be more true if it is the last child. Much has been written and said about the empty-nest syndrome. It is probably not a syndrome in the classical use of that term. However, it is certainly a force to be reckoned with. Too often parents build their own mutual relationship around the children rather than each other. Unfortunately, they even sometimes interact through the children. Obviously, when the children exit, it leaves the marriage in a precarious condition. Many divorces occur around that time. So, the leaving-home crisis is often more severe for parents than teens.

As a result of the multiple and complex phenomena occurring during late adolescence, the teenager is often chronically tense or frustrated. The possibility of beginning college or entering full-time employment is not only exciting but new. It is frightening and sometimes intimidating. In the midst of all this upheaval, the entire family can make some bad decisions.

A CASE OF LEAVING HOME

Jack was a senior in high school. He had experienced little adjustment or parental difficulty through his junior year. During the summer preceding his senior year he got a job selling used computers. He succeeded quite well and made a substantial sum of money. In fact, during the summer months alone he earned more than $4,000. He had not wanted to return to school his senior year, yet did so at the insistence of his parents and employer. They would not allow anything else. In fact, his employer told Jack in spite of high sales that he could not use him after August if he refused to return to school.

Jack considered his parents' comments manipulative and insulting but never really discussed it. He returned to school with a great deal of money and an illusion that he could probably survive without a high school education. His behavior at school and at home soon began to decline. In April of his senior year he and his father became involved in an intense argument. Impulsively, his father told Jack that if he didn't want to obey the rules he could just leave.

Jack did.

Three weeks later, still living separately, the family came into counseling. Eventually, Jack returned home and then left a year later on a more cordial basis.

LEAVING HOME AS DEVELOPMENTAL STAGE

Leaving home is almost a ritual. It is vital that adolescents proceed through this stage successfully. Leaving home successfully implies doing so on reasonably good terms with parents. It includes the parents' "blessing" and their emotional support. The adolescent needs to know that his family is rooting for him and that he always has a nest he can return to if necessary. Such a process requires a great deal of discussion and planning to occur successfully. Parents need to initiate the appropriate conversations and supervise the planning of a successful departure.

The leaving-home crisis most often occurs during the senior year of high school. At times it appears that some teenagers do everything they can to avoid graduating. I have worked with many teens who subconsciously fear the unknown of leaving home. In response to that they create obstacles to graduation, without really knowing why. That would effectively put off the crisis period, in their minds. Parents need to be especially attentive to their teenagers during late adolescent years. The willingness to listen with open expression is excellent preventive medicine.

DANGERS OF HANGING ON

Reaching the age of eighteen or the senior year of high school does not necessarily mean one is emotionally prepared to face leaving home. Incidentally, it is also untrue that simply because a child reaches six years of age he needs to enter the first grade. Sometimes that is accomplished at a later and more emotionally appropriate age.

However, parents cannot hold an adolescent emotionally hostage without negative effects. That may happen when parents are not prepared to face the empty nest. The result is an overly dependent late adolescent who is not allowed to complete the developmental stage necessary for adulthood. This easily leads to various forms of emotional handicaps. In some cases it has led to depression and even suicide attempts.

Even though hanging on too long is often an unconscious process entered into by well-meaning parents, it is nonetheless destructive. Most people who visit me on a professional basis and most parents I know have impeccably good intentions. However, the outcome of those intentions can possibly be damaging to a teenager. That is often the case during a leaving-home stage. The family may have some difficulty when any child leaves home. However, the youngest or only child is in greatest jeopardy of the leaving-home crisis.

It is impossible to state an age at which an adolescent should be independent. Naturally the temptation is to desire specific and concrete guidelines. Yet, the age of an individual capable of, and ready for, successful independence varies with personal differences. A son or daughter may attempt leaving home only to return later when a job falls through or a marriage folds.

However, just as we create problems by kicking out a child too early, we can do the same by hanging on too long. By fostering dependence in the late adolescent, we create problems for the child. There are various ways of doing that. The problem is made more difficult because of the parents' attitude of love and concern for the child. Sometimes, however, parental love can prevent the late adolescent from negotiating some important developmental stages.

One of the important qualities for late teens to learn is self-responsibility. That involves a number of things but can be generalized as learning the skills and attitude characterized by the sentence "if it is to be, it's up to me." Small things can contribute to an attitude of self-responsibility. A late teenager needs to be able to take care of personal hygiene, do laundry, and earn a portion of money needed for self-support. Basically, the late teenager needs to be moving toward an independent, self-supporting life-style. Many teens (especially boys) become passive observers of life, supported and cared for by loving mothers. Columnist Lewis Grizzard mentions that he discovered many things after leaving "Mamma" and getting married. Until marriage, he thought that when an article of clothing was thrown on the floor, it grew legs and walked to the clothes hamper. Apparently he discovered the truth too late!

Adolescents who grow up overly dependent on parents have difficulty making the transition into independent adulthood. We can probably ease that process by allowing teens to experience the logical consequences of their behavior. As an example, if a late adolescent threw his clothes on the floor, they would not grow legs and walk away. In fact, the clothes would remain there until the teenager decided to pick them up. If one refused to iron his clothes, he would wear wrinkled ones. If he decided not to do his homework, he would be allowed to fail the class and repeat it the following year.

Sometimes the best thing a parent can do is to let go of a child. Hanging on too long in one case created a forty-one-year-old adolescent. Personally, I want my children to be through their teen years a little before that!

The goal of adolescence is to encourage a responsible degree of self-sufficiency in the late stages so that children can continue their lives successfully beyond leaving home and even beyond death of parents. If the family has a crisis or question during the leaving-home period, it is probably best to seek professional help.

FOR FURTHER THOUGHT

1. As a teenager, how did you express anger? Were you allowed to express it openly? Was sharing of emotion encouraged or discouraged in some way? Who encouraged or discouraged it? How did you feel toward that person?

2. Recall the kind of modeling you observed in your parents or guardians. Were they able to express emotions, including anger, in a positive way? Consider how anger was expressed in your home. Was it expressed openly or in some indirect manner?

3. How do you feel when you observe someone acting out anger or expressing anger openly? Do you shrink away? Do you want to run? Are you grateful for their openness, and do you encourage it for the purpose of working through it?

4. Think of one particular teenager. How do you see him or her handling anger and other emotions? Is he willing to express it and talk it out? Does he withdraw, shut himself away? Does he slam doors or become violent? Are grades, clothing, or hairdos used as a means of expression of anger?

5. What are you doing to teach others how to handle anger in a positive, mature way? Does their anger kindle yours until both of you erupt? How can you model for them an acceptable, healthy way to deal with the honest emotion of anger?

My beloved brethren. . . . let everyone be quick to hear, slow to speak and slow to anger.

—James 1:19

There is a certain relief in change, even though it be from bad to worse; as I have found in travelling in a stagecoach, that it is often a comfort to shift one's position and be bruised in a new place.

—Washington Irving, *Tales of a Traveller*

7

SELF-DESTRUCTIVENESS: RECOGNIZING CRIES FOR HELP

EXCERPT: LETTER FROM MOTHER OF SUICIDE VICTIM 1981

"April had always seemed alone. She had friends, but even when with them there was something lonely about her. As a baby it was almost as if she didn't want us to touch her. We got her when she was only three weeks old. But maybe there just wasn't the bonding there was with her brother.

"I felt sorry for her. She seemed continuously forlorn. After my husband left it probably started going downhill. She got hurt at school the very week he left us. It just seemed from then on there was always something wrong. Her grades got terrible. She got thrown out of a friend's car. She broke her leg playing softball and broke her nose playing volleyball. She was just accident-prone.

"She never had a real boyfriend after the third grade. I don't know why. I guess she was just so moody all the time that nobody wanted to be with her. In the seventh grade I discovered that she was having sex with older boys. I know she still sneaked out once in a while afterwards. That probably was when she started using drugs. I really don't know all that she did. Lisa, one of her friends, had told me they took diet pills and that April occasionally got some other drugs at school. She was just a lonely child.

"The last week I should have noticed the changes, but looking backward is always easier. She was writing a lot of poetry. Of course she always had. I didn't look until afterwards. The poetry was about death and the devil. It was gruesome. She gave Lisa about all of her records, which was strange, but I didn't think much about it at the time. April's classmates said that she had seemed unusually happy at school that Friday. Later I remembered our discussion that we had had about death the Wednesday before. It was almost like she used to be. We thought she was better. Saturday, when I finally went into her room, she was lying in the bed. She had died from an overdose. She must have been saving the pills up for a long time. The report said that she had taken the exact combination and dosage to kill peacefully. It seemed to be fully planned with her last will and testament in her letter to me. . . ."

SIGNS AND SIGNALS

People in pain will give off signals. Sometimes the signals are obvious. A person who gets cut bleeds. Someone who breaks a leg limps. An infection will result in increased temperature, even a fever.

Emotional pain is usually not as obvious, especially in teenagers. There are likely to be signals, even with adolescents, but occasionally they are so vague we miss them. Yet they are there and very important. These "calls" for help may be the fail-safe mechanism referred to earlier.

After reading this book, anyone will be able to look back at April's letter and see some very clear signals and self-destructive behavior. Yet, occurring as slowly as they did with her, they would be easy to miss. Over the course of this chapter, certain forms of self-destructive behavior are discussed. After looking at this chapter, it might be interesting to return to the letter and read it again. Some cries are louder than others.

DEEP CALLS FOR HELP

Self-destructiveness in any form can be viewed as a call for help. Some of these behaviors can be dramatic and rather obvious. Others may be more subtle or disguised. As parents we are not expected to be mindreaders. However, there is a responsibility to be present for the adolescent if for no other reason than simply to observe. In fact, observing adolescents when they are unaware is one of the most reliable indicators of whether or not they are in emotional trouble. Certain observations or reports concerning adolescent behavior can be interpreted as a call for help. This is expecially important if self-destructiveness of any kind is a trend. These isolated signals may or may not be significant. The true danger is observing them in combination. Some experts say if two or more signals persist longer than two weeks a response should be made.

WITHDRAWAL

Withdrawal is not always self-destructive. If it is severe, or if it continues for an extended period of time, it can be a signal. This includes such things as withdrawal from people as well as from habits or objects. As an example, decreasing grades could be indicative of withdrawal from school. Unwillingness to speak to family members is withdrawing from family. The classical withdrawal is found in one who retreats to his room and sleeps incessantly. That is often accompanied by complaints of being chronically fatigued or tired.

Any adolescent is going to be tired, if for no other reason than because of the growth and changes he or she is experiencing. However, excessive or unrealistic fatigue can by symptomatic of depression and should be looked at closely. Certainly overt withdrawal and an appearance of being physically depressed is a clear danger signal. In that case, immediate professional help should be sought.

INAPPROPRIATE SEXUAL BEHAVIOR

Adolescents can become involved in inappropriate sexual relationships as a means of sedating feelings of severe depression. Those relationships are sometimes a result of an adolescent's continually searching for a measure of unconditional acceptance.

Most parents perceive inappropriate sexual behavior as mere "rebellion" and place restrictions on the acting out teenager. Less than satisfactory results usually occur for both parents and teen. Overtly sexual behavior is usually a symptom of underlying problems, and these are the issues the parents need to address.

ACCIDENT-PRONENESS

Accident-proneness can indeed be a response to the growth spurt and other hormonal changes occurring during the adolescent period. Equally, it can be a result of continued reinforcement from attention given immediately after the accident.

My eldest son developed a way to get my attention several years ago. He would sneak up to me and bite my toe. At first I thought it was cute and would call my wife. He was only a toddler, and I thought anything he did was cute. I responded so actively to his bite that he thought he had discovered something of a phenomenal nature. He bit it perhaps two other times, during which I laughed.

I soon realized the response I had created. By rewarding him with intense attention for biting my toe I had strengthened the likelihood that he would continue to bite. The only way to extinguish the behavior would be to ignore his biting.

Predictably he soon bit my toe again. I held my breath and squinted. No response. He looked up at me smiling. I ignored it.

He bit again and then looked expectantly at me for a laugh. Nothing.

He tried a third time, still no response. Deciding that didn't work, he crawled into my lap and said, "Let's play, Daddy." I responded enthusiastically. A new behavior was strengthened.

If the only time a child gets attention is when he catches the measles or breaks his leg, that sort of behavior is likely to be repeated. It is certainly one way to learn accident-proneness.

In that way, accident-proneness during later adolescence can indeed be a cry for help or a cry for attention.

UNSAFE DRIVING HABITS

Automobile accidents are the leading cause of death among adolescents aged fifteen to twenty-four. Continuous inappropriate or unsafe driving habits can certainly be an example of self-destructive behavior. Such behavior should be observed to determine if it is indeed a cry for help.

Unsafe habits can be observed as early as kindergarten when a child becomes careless on a tricycle. Proper habits can be taught by parents at this early age. Late adolescence, however, is certainly not too late to begin proper driving habits. One study found that requiring adolescent traffic offenders to write essays, explaining and analyzing their mistakes, was much more effective a deterrent to repeated offenses than other consequences, such as fining and restriction of driving privileges. Restricting driving privileges was, in fact, found to be counterproductive.

Certainly, parents should take strong responsible action when an adolescent demonstrates blatant irresponsibility in driving habits. Yet, even more important is the willingness to observe the adolescent and listen for signals of what is wrong. In any case, before jumping to conclusions, a parent should express love and concern and give the teenager time to explain his behavior.

Several years ago, as a new marriage and family counselor, I worked in a small clinic in southern California. One morning before going to the office I received a phone call from my secretary. Her voice was strained and tense. After a few seconds of uneasy silence she finally explained.

"I have no idea how to tell you this. You just need to come on in here, probably. I need to talk to you."

My mind raced with possibilities. I had no idea what was troubling her. I quickly went down the list of options, rejecting each. I wasn't on call, so it probably wasn't an emergency case.

"Betty, what's going on?" I finally asked. "I'm working late tonight. I'm not supposed to come in until this afternoon." I waited for an answer.

"John. It's bad. It's Terry Jones. He got killed in a car wreck last night." She stopped speaking, but her voice trailed off. I knew there was more she had to say.

"Mr. Jones has locked himself up in his office and won't let anyone come in. Mrs. Jones wants to talk to you about what to do."

I was devastated. I had worked closely with this family and had become well acquainted with them. Terry was a tremendous youngster. He was an athlete, a good student, and very likable. His parents were both kind and loving people. Yet, as with any family, there were problems.

Terry had been picked up for driving while intoxicated five different times. On each occasion, his father, the district attorney, had gotten Terry out of legal difficulty without even as much as a ticket. Terry never had to pay any consequences. His father's behavior had created difficulty in the family. Mrs. Jones had been irate when she discovered what had occurred. Her husband had hidden it, even from her.

They both loved Terry without any reservation. However, each expressed his love uniquely. Terry once had told me the only time his dad ever spent time with him was when he got "picked up." Mr. Jones didn't seem to understand the significance of that comment.

Mr. Jones was giving Terry implied permission to drive drunk. A responsible action would have been to let his son lose his driving privileges and for the two of them to spend time together in a personal relationship.

It's too late.

I still weep for this family, literally. I figuratively weep for any family who fails to recognize cries for help.

DRUG ABUSE

Alcohol is the number one drug of abuse among adolescents today. Parental influence and media attention are only two of various factors affecting that. It is estimated that upwards of 90 percent of adolescent boys and 86 percent of adolescent girls will at some point experiment with alcohol. That is a statistical reality, and the trend continues. Many parents act surprised to discover their adolescent has experimented with beer. Actually, drinking is all too common.

Parents can give subtle approval to drinking, perceiving it as a safer alternative to other drugs. Advertisers spend literally millions of dollars annually on beer commercials and advertisements. As a result of all those influences the American Medical Association suggests that if current trends continue, probably one out of fifteen adolescents today will become alcoholic before age eighteen.

Alcoholism and other drug abuse is a drastic signal that help is needed. In fact, it should be considered an alarm. Our country is filled today with facilities specializing in treating adolescents who have difficulty with drugs. Skilled staffs in those facilities are able to sensitively help adolescents and parents in dealing with these complex problems.

EATING DISORDERS

Similar to alcohol and drug addiction, eating disorders such as anorexia or bulimia can be perceived as alarms for help. Such afflictions are in many ways systematic and methodical versions of suicide and should be viewed as serious.

Obsessive compulsive disorders of this nature should be treated not only by professionals but by experts who have specialized training in this area. There are now both inpatient and outpatient facilities nationally that exclusively treat eating disorders among adolescents.

DEPRESSION

As explained in chapter 4 there are various symptoms of depression, some subtle and others not. One logical conclusion of a depressive trend could be death. Depression can be a slow and extremely painful form of suicide. The more serious forms of depression such as catatonia and psychotic depression are almost coma-like. Reactions such as these occur almost insidiously, which is primarily why they are so easily overlooked.

With adolescents, the symptoms must be observed in the early stages. Intervention needs to occur as soon as possible. The later intervention is made, the graver the outcome. It would be wise for parents to completely familiarize themselves with early symptoms and to respond as needed when those symptoms are observed in combination. Any one of those behaviors, alone and observed only for brief periods, may be quite normal. But if several of the behaviors are observed in one adolescent, there may be reason to respond quickly with professional help.

AGGRESSION

Simply put, some aggressiveness is likely during adolescence, especially in boys. If uncontrolled fighting or aggressive behavior persists, there is cause to be alarmed.

Certain forms of aggressive behavior are probably healthy. Much of organized athletics is based on the principle of controlled aggression. Paradoxically, that can be useful in socialization and in teaching an adolescent the value of teamwork and cooperation.

This is contrasted with any kind of uncontrolled aggression or destructive behavior. Fighting, destroying things, or any preoccupation with violence needs to be responded to quickly. Such behavior can be extremely dangerous and even deadly toward the adolescent or others. It is indeed self-destructive and often a signal that help is needed.

MELODRAMA

Occasionally, adolescents will resort to dramatic gestures that could be interpreted as cries for help. Some people refer to such melodrama as "acting out." It may be that these behaviors are also demands for paternal intervention.

One puzzled parent presented his daughter's diary to me. She had left it open to a particular page, lying on her father's bathroom floor. When he glanced at the entry, it described an orgy his teenager had hosted with sex, drugs, and a live rock band. At first he was overwhelmed. But when he looked at the date, he realized that was when the entire family, including his daughter, were together on vacation. Other entries describing similar adventures also had conflicting dates. He had no idea what to believe.

The parents of a seventeen-year-old boy reported similar confusion. He regularly reported stories of being shot at, chased by police, and followed by the CIA. Their son was an extremely intelligent adolescent and convincing in his stories. They had finally decided to enter counseling after discovering he had wiretapped their bedroom.

The parents of an eighteen-year-old were not only troubled but alarmed at their daughter's trend toward melodrama. She had called different crisis counseling centers and at various times accused her father, her pastor, and medical doctor of raping her. Each accusation had been formally investigated by legal authorities and proved untrue, yet the family had suffered tremendous stress and pain.

Each of those teenagers was acting out of the pain and loneliness experienced within. Adolescence is a lonely and sometimes sadistic stage of life. Popular songs have lamented the trauma and occasional cruelty teens put each other through. Occasionally the only retreat is into a world where fantasy is preferable to reality. And attention from imagination is better than none at all.

This behavior can range from entertaining and harmless to frightening and severe in its consequences. Melodrama can be a cry for help or a way to get attention. The more severe drama probably requires professional attention.

OTHER SIGNALS

One study of suicide trends illustrated that loss combined with a presence of aggressiveness and depression could result in multiple suicide attempts. This was even more significant if the combination was absent of any professional attention. It would be certain then that this constellation of symptoms could be perceived as a red flag by concerned adults.

Another study of suicide attempters found that severe punishment during childhood may be a determinate of later suicide attempts by adolescents. Basically the child would learn to treat himself as others have and become self-punishing. As a child grows, the self-punishment would precede punishment from others. In the confused adolescent mind, that would be obstensibly for the purpose of gaining parental approval.

Another study points out that an adolescent who has made a decision to take his own life may be in a remarkably calm state immediately before the event. This is sometimes misinterpreted even among professionals as a sign of improvement. This "calm before the storm" reflects a sense of peace within the tortured adolescent. The decision has been made in the adolescent's mind, and the pain will soon be over. This is an extremely dangerous state and is in all reality the last opportunity to intervene. Although this condition may be one of total silence, it is the loudest of all deep calls.

CONTRIBUTING FACTORS

Other things must be considered when thinking of just what can be interpreted as a suicide danger sign. Researchers have found 70 percent of all teen suicides had alcohol in their systems. Fifty percent had experienced recent physical altercations. Essentially all had exhibited some form of disruptive behavior prior to the attempt. These included such clear signals as truancy, promiscuity, temper outbursts, physical illness, or excessive drug abuse.

It is impossible to ignore the fact that most suicide attempters are from single-parent homes. However, that does not comment on the quality of the single-parent family. What it does indeed comment on is the lack of adult relationships caused by the departed parent's absence. That dynamic also exists when considering the "psychologically absent" father. An example is the case of one who is so involved in his work or own success that he virtually ignores his children. The maternal equivalent is the seductive narcissistic mother who is overly domineering of both husband and children. Either case is maladaptive and can create various problems for their children.

FOR FURTHER THOUGHT

1. Review the "cries for help" in this chapter. Do you recall ever experiencing any of them yourself during your own adolescence? What were you trying to say? What kinds of responses did you get? From whom?

2. As an adult, review what your needs are today. Contrast how in touch you are now and when you were a teen. Have you overlooked an unfulfilled need? Why? How does your response make you feel? What will you do about it?

3. Review the kinds of trouble signals that could be sent by a teenager you know without easy detection. What changes would you observe in this teenager? Write out the response you would make.

4. Are there subjects you feel uneasy discussing with teenagers? Analyze the origin of your uneasiness.

5. Go back over April's letter. How many danger signals do you detect now? Do you note similar signals in any teen you know? What will you do about it?

6. Think of any self-destructive behavior you may be involved in as an adult. Overeating or not exercising may be an example. Analyze the reasons why you might continue the behavior even if it is destructive.

Why are you in despair, O my soul? And why are you disturbed within me?

—Psalm 43:5

If I had to choose between pain and nothing, I would always choose pain.

—William Faulkner

8

THE TRAUMA OF
SUICIDE ATTEMPTS

The Trauma of Suicide

E ven at their best, suicide attempts are devastating to the family and the victim. Successful suicides are even more damaging. The emotional trauma experienced by family and friends ranges from extreme guilt to denial, rage, and profound anguish. People blame themselves for not noticing. Eventually they even blame each other as the reality becomes more confusing. It is quite common for families of both unsuccessful and successful suicide attempts to eventually experience depression themselves and occasionally additional attempts.

Many people who attempt suicide do so under the misconception that it will "make things better." In my professional experience I am aware of no cases where that has been true.

THE TRAUMA OF THE ATTEMPT

Patty had been caught.

Her parents were waiting for her as she arrived home. She glanced at her watch. It was 3:15 A.M. She was more than four hours late. Admittedly, it really wasn't her fault.

And she could not have predicted the car problems. But it had been fun, and there was no way she could have contacted her parents. She thanked the others as she got out of the car and encouraged them to drive on. They all knew her parents would be upset.

Mrs. Potts did not know whether to be relieved or angry. She experienced a mixture of both emotions as Patty walked up the driveway. Her husband opened the door trying to get a glimpse of the car as it sped away. In his hand he held Patty's diary. He had been reading it earlier, searching for a clue indicating where she might be. He had quite a few questions for Patty. Many of them came from her diary entries.

Patty came up the front steps dreading the confrontation she knew had to occur.

"Daddy, I'm sorry. There were some problems. We had an accident. The police came, and then we had to wait. I tried to call you. Nobody was hurt but—what is that? My diary? What have you been doing with my diary?"

"It's almost 3:30, Patty. We called the police. Your brother and Tim are out looking for you. We have been sick with worry. Where have you been?"

Patty acted as if she hadn't heard her father's question.

"Why do you have my diary? Did you read it?"

"Of course we read it. We were trying to find out where you might be. I have some questions for you about it, too. But where in the world have you been?"

"You read my diary. I hate you! How could you have done that? Oh, no!" She screamed at both her parents and ran into the bathroom.

"I'll get even with them," she thought to herself. Patty jerked open the medicine cabinet and started taking every pill she could find.

Her parents banged desperately on the door, but Patty ignored them. In a frenzy, she gulped down every available pill. She drank the contents of different bottles including her father's aftershave. In a moment, her dad had broken in the door.

Patty stopped and stared at them. She suddenly realized for the first time what she had done.

"Oh, please, Daddy. Don't let me die! I'm sorry."

She felt nauseous as her body lapsed into unconsciousness. The following day she woke up. The hospital room was unfamiliar, but her mother's face was both a friendly and welcome sight.

TRAUMA OF RECOVERY

The pain and work began at this point. Patty's parents were obviously glad she was alive. Their emotions, however, alternated between joy at her surviving and horror at what she had attempted.

Her hospitalization lasted almost two weeks. After receiving general medical care, Patty was referred for psychiatric evaluation and treatment. Some six weeks later the parents visited me for family counseling.

By this time Patty's younger sister had become depressed and had been suspended from school for drug use. The parents were plagued by guilt, anger, and confusion. Patty's older brother had refused to speak to her since the attempt. As a group, the family was tense and frustrated.

It took several visits before the family could all sit in the same room for an entire counseling session. The emotional barriers prevented them from even making eye contact. I visited with this family periodically for more than seven months. Before the counseling process was completed, Patty's younger sister had also attempted suicide. Her mother was hospitalized for serious depression. Patty eventually ran away but was returned to the family. Her father almost lost his job because of absenteeism.

Over time the family began recovering. Patty's suicide attempt did not provide any answers or solutions. It helped nothing. Patty has told literally hundreds of others through the years that suicide is not the answer. The trauma she and her family have experienced is a good example.

A LOGICAL ACT

Patty's suicide attempt was not as impulsive as it first appeared. She had a long history of emotional problems that ultimately led to a decision to even the score with her parents. Her behavior also effectively neutralized the issue of the curfew violation.

Most suicide attempts are even more methodical and logical than hers. To the victims, it is a process they have considered at length. Various options have been examined. Suicide to them, as with Patty, is viewed as a tension reducer. The choice is then made. Most cases of which I have personal knowledge were decided in a similar manner. At the time committed, it appeared impulsive. At a closer glance, however, it does not.

PURPOSE—A CONTRIBUTION TO HOPE

Nobody can pinpoint factors that lead one person to choose death and another life. So far, it has been impossible to isolate concrete evidence of contributing factors. Some say that the primary consideration should be biochemical. Indeed, in laboratory research it has been discovered that some suicide victims have lower levels of serotonin (a chemical found in the blood that helps regulate mood) than the normal population. Others indicate that it is socioeconomic. Someone else has suggested that it depends on the strength of the social network. Research has been unable to prove anything conclusively. However, it can reflect certain trends. Perhaps personal experience can also provide some insight.

Viktor Frankl is an Austrian psychiatrist and author. During World War II he survived the Nazi concentration camp at Auschwitz. His observations were that those with a sense of purpose were the ones who survived the horror. For some, purpose meant living so they could bring their persecutors to justice. For others, purpose meant living long enough to see a country born. Others found purpose in living long enough for the Allies to come. Those who lost or had no purpose simply gave up and died.

Perhaps the philosophical opposite of purpose is hopelessness. That is indeed one common thread connecting those who attempt and especially those who succeed at suicide. The roots of such hopelessness are unknown.

The importance of parental and other adult relationships has already been established. We do know that the largest proportion of those adolescents who attempt suicide report feeling an absence of warmth toward significant adult figures. In fact, the majority of suicide attempters report never experiencing any sense of love or warmth toward an adult.

Perhaps this hopelessness is connected to the lack of a sense of love in those who eventually end their lives. To date, research shows there is no evidence to prove that. It is merely thought for discussion. However, considering the reports by suicide attempters, we may have stumbled upon a strong clue in support of that possibility. Adolescents are comforted when they believe they can depend on an adults for strength and resources other than their own. The large number of those who feel a lack of warmth toward adults may be a significant factor to consider.

A similar comfort is found in many adults and teens who have a belief in God. It gives them an added reservoir of strength that others don't have. We know from experience that adolescents who have a poor relationship with parents usually have a poor relationship with God. The adult relationship in many ways is actually a model for the relationship with God. If it is absent, then the adolescent not only has reduced his reservoir of resources but also is less likely to have a trusting relationship with God. Thus the possibility of gaining hope from that source is reduced. That is one possibile origin of hopelessness.

MEDIA INFLUENCE

A recent news magazine reported that a Milwaukee man set his estranged wife on fire after viewing a TV movie about a battered wife who burned her husband to death. Three weeks after the release of the movie *An Officer and a Gentleman*, at least three teenagers were found dead, hanged from a shower in a manner similar to one of the characters in the movie. One week after another TV movie and a popular magazine cover issue on teen suicide, a seventeen-year-old ended her life in identical manner to the teens in the movie. She had carried the magazine issue with her that entire week and discussed the movie with all of her friends.

The media has a major impact on teens today. To ignore the power of the media is folly. Television, radio, and the press have the eyes and ears of adolescents. Look at a recent list of heroes. You will find movie stars, musicians, and other media celebrities. The day when athletes and government leaders led the roster of heroes has long passed.

One front-page headline of a national newspaper declared that the average American home has a television on six and one-half hours per day. The average teenage stereo is probably on for a similar amount of time. Therefore, parents need to not only stay informed but responsive to media influence. It is essential to be aware of who and what has predominance over our young people. The media resources need to be used, not smugly ignored. It is virtually impossible to insulate a teenager from the power of media influence.

UTILIZATION OF MEDIA

Katie was on time for her appointment. She had been a suicide attempter. I had worried about her over the weekend and was relieved to see her usual smile.

"This is Tommy, my new boyfriend. Will you let him come in with me?"

"Sure. But let's talk alone for a few minutes before Tommy joins us. How does it feel to be a star?" I teased.

"That's part of what he's here for."

"OK," I hesitated.

At my request, Katie had agreed to be interviewed by a local TV station. We had cooperated in response to a network special on teen suicide. I had done several interviews for them. One of those included blacked-out reports of Katie and another adolescent, Laura, who had also attempted suicide. The young ladies had readily agreed to the interviews, but I worried about their friends recognizing them (even though they were blacked out and their voices were changed).

In fact, Katie had been recognized by a few friends. But in her opinion it gave her more opportunity to help others. Now, however, she was concerned about Tommy. The night before, after watching the network special on teen suicide, he had wanted to talk to his mother. Apparently, he had been depressed for quite some time and had recently considered suicide as a viable alternative.

Tommy, his mother, and stepfather watched the special together. Tommy had responded with open emotion both to the special and the local report that followed. After the news report, he turned off the TV and asked his mother if they could talk. She responded that she was sleepy and suggested that they speak to each other in the morning before school.

Tommy was overwhelmed with rejection by that response. For weeks he had wanted to talk to her. He was upset about school, was angry with his father, and felt ignored by his mother since her remarriage. And now this. In his mind it was hopeless.

He went to his bedroom and decided to take his life. First he called Katie to say "good night." She detected something in his voice. After hanging up, she drove immediately to his house. They talked until 4:00 A.M. Tommy agreed not to commit suicide. After school that day she had brought him to my office.

Tommy's mother had missed an important opportunity. No doubt she had legitimate reasons for asking to delay discussion. Yet as parents we need to be sensitive to such key moments. Left unprocessed, his concern and confusion could have been a truly deadly combination. The TV movie had allowed some of Tommy's negative thoughts to surface. Those thoughts needed to be shared at that moment. In this case, the power of the media teetered between positive and negative. The deciding vote was the response of his mother. Fortunately, an attentive friend saved his life. It was almost lost because of the combination of a powerful media and an unaware parent.

Many times we miss opportunities. Rather than try to ignore television in this case, the mother could have utilized it positively. Eventually she did. I spent the remainder of my time that day with Tommy and Katie. He entered counseling soon thereafter and today has renewed resources of hope.

ROMANTICIZING SUICIDE

In Elton John's record album *Honky Chateau,* one song is entitled "I Think I'm Gonna Kill Myself." The lyrics recite many of the problems teens face. Family problems, parental restrictions, and some of the confusion of adolescence are poetically recited to music.

The theme song of one of the country's all-time favorite TV shows claims "suicide is painless." Fortunately the lyrics of that theme are not sung.

In a reported response to Pink Floyd's album *The Wall,* two teenagers in Seattle crashed their car into a wall as part of a mutual suicide agreement. In the note they left behind, the album was reported as a factor in their death pact.

Any influence of the media that romanticizes suicide or makes it appear easy is part of the problem. That is a fine line to draw and probably an unfair one to place on the media. Certainly parents share the responsibility. As in the case of Tommy, it could have gone either way. It depended on the response of his mother. However, because of the power and impact of the media, it shares the responsibility to present a fair picture to the adolescent. Even more helpful are the efforts of those who attempt to harness the power of media to productive use. Many radio and television stations across the country are such resources today.

An excellent example is the effort of the media to assist in teenage suicide crisis. The Missing Children's Network is also a gesture of helpful involvement. There are probably hundreds of other examples that could illustrate the powerful positive use of the media.

SUICIDE: PRECIPITATING FACTORS

Suicide is sometimes an attempt to "get even" with parents, spouses, or someone else. It is attempted at other times as a result of a sense of hopelessness. At still other times it is a result of the loss of love. In all those cases it is usually (as pointed out before) the result of a long series of events resulting in chronic depression. The loss, or vindictiveness, usually functions as a precipitating event.

Occasionally, suicide is viewed as a method of reducing anxiety. The anxiety can be a result of interpersonal conflict, loneliness, or even sickness. Many times the anxiety is so great that death seems a better alternative.

People who have lived with a chronic sense of worthlessness may choose a slower, more methodical method of ending their lives. The diabetic who refuses to take his insulin is a possibile example. Similar examples are the victim of lung disease who continues to smoke cigarettes; the alcoholic who persists in drinking; or the anorexic who refuses to eat. These people may be actually slowly reducing the anxiety of everyday emotional turmoil in their own minds. One way to do that is through a slow death.

A LEARNED BEHAVIOR

Suicide, similar to depression, can be a learned or modeled behavior. Children of suicide attempters are more likely to attempt it themselves. The presence of depression in the parents was stated earlier as being a more significant predictor of suicide attempts than in previous attempts by the same person. In other words, weighing a parent's depression on one side and a child's previous suicidal attempt on the other, the parent's depression would actually outweigh the latter as influencing a child toward a possible second attempt.

The possibility exists that adolescents learn how to deal with anger, disappointment, and other emotions by observing their parents. If a parent internalizes emotions, represses feelings, and avoids expressiveness, so will the child. These adolescents are discouraged by their parents from dealing openly with pain. And soon they become depressed. The adolescent often begins then to take on the parent's load of depression, and hopelessness sets in. Thus, suicide can become a viable option.

THE FLIP SIDE OF SUICIDE

Researchers have primarily focused on the aspect of who commits suicide. There is a need to also look at who does not. Those who avoid suicide have at least some of the following characteristics in common. They include a higher degree of self-esteem and a healthy sense of self; good health and an active life-style; a rewarding family life and strong parental and other adult relationships; a social network of friends; involvement in a supportive church; and freedom from debilitating emotional confusion. That is a good summary of goals for a family to use as targets for which to aim.

THE MCKNIGHT FAMILY

The McKnights are one example of a family in which children did not become depressed or attempt suicide. Jane is now twenty-three and married. Mark and Jack are twenty-one and nineteen, respectively, and both are in college. The mother and father are highly functioning people in their own right. He is forty-seven, and she is two years younger.

Mr. and Mrs. McKnight did make mistakes as parents. They also admitted those mistakes and apologized to their children when they occurred. Parents and children alike were allowed to openly express their emotions, both positive and negative. Sometimes, people even flew off the handle. They were not punished for expressing their anger, but there were logical consequences for breaking certain family rules.

Each child was allowed to have a unique identity. No pressure to perform or unrealistic expectations were placed on the family by other family members. When one of the teens decided not to go to church, it was discussed and then the parents took turns staying home with the teen until he decided on his own to return. The children were given responsibility for doing their own homework and making grades. They also were allowed to choose if they would go to public or private school. They discussed such matters with their parents and received a great deal of encouragement.

The children all chose to be athletic. The parents made a special effort to encourage and support their choices. Dad missed work occasionally to attend ball games. Two days a week they all exercised together.

The children had a variety of adult friends while they were growing up. Dad made that possible without their realizing what he was doing. Occasionally, when the boys became angry at each other or at their parents, it was arranged for them to spend a night or two with these other families. The parents also made an extra effort to make friends with their teenagers' friends. On occasion those friends would talk to them about problems the McKnight children were having. One of the children did have emotional conflicts during a stage of his life. The parents let him choose with whom he would like to discuss the problem. He chose the football coach. After checking it out with the coach, the parents gave their approval.

The McKnights never criticized their teens or punished them with fear and guilt. They also refrained from comparing them with each other. Dad spanked the eldest child once in her entire life. He later said it was his mistake and not hers. The other two were never spanked. The McKnights cared about their children deeply and expressed it often and openly. The entire family openly demonstrated affection. They are the kind of people you enjoy being around.

I still visit them every chance I get. They make me feel good about being alive.

SURVIVORS

Guilt has become a characteristic response to suicide. One young lady reported that her parents ignored her three weeks after her suicide attempt and actually refused to speak to her. Family guilt over successful suicides is even greater. In fact it is so excessive that people sometimes do not overcome it for years. Survivors are often filled and occasionally overcome with self-blame. They condemn their lack of attentiveness at noticing the symptoms and blame themselves or others.

Some people can develop physical illness following the suicide of a relative. That is usually because of the stress that accompanies such a death. It may last the entire bereavement period. That period unfortunately can continue indefinitely. A child suicide often results in the divorce of surviving parents or the splitting of other family members.

Parents may continue to feel inappropriately responsible for the adolescent death long beyond the normal period of grief that would be attached to it. Society is often of little assistance and in reality lacks understanding of the family's needs. Sadly, there seems to be a typical response by society that the family must have done something wrong. There is a long history of mythology concerning suicide, which is discussed in a later chapter.

It would not only be appropriate but vital in the case of a suicide attempt or of a successful suicide that professional assistance be sought. A trained psychotherapist or pastoral counselor can assist any family in organizing or reorganizing in the wake of such a crisis. This is a difficult period that must be dealt with carefully.

Those of us who are observers of the family trauma need to be sensitive and responsive. Obviously, at someone's death it is normal and actually healthy to grieve. Expressions of caring, warmth, and empathy can be most helpful. Rather than simply offering assistance or saying, "If I can do anything call," it is better to do something! That is usually more appreciated than even the most sincere verbal offer of assistance. Basic tasks need to be accomplished. Simple items such as lawnmowing, automobile care, or snow shoveling need to be done. Sometimes, merely taking care of a similar mundane task is more helpful than anything else.

In the case of unsuccessful attempts at suicide, nonfamily can be indispensable. Under these circumstances, verbal and nonverbal expressions of understanding are usually welcomed. Such gestures are appropriate to both family and the survivor.

After time has passed, encouraging family discussion and getting actively involved with the survivor is both beneficial and constructive. Introducing the survivor into social networks and self-esteem building activity may prevent future crisis.

EMOTIONAL FIRST AID

In response to a suicide attempt or any other crisis, it is important to first observe. Open all sensory channels. Look, listen, smell, and touch if necessary. Only after you have some sense of understanding as to what the nature of the crisis is, is a response appropriate.

Express concern and love for the person. Try to introduce hope into their lives. Reassure them that everything is going to be OK, even if the outlook is grim. As a helper, keep your individual response under control. Try to appear calm, even if inwardly you are churning. Breathe deeply and slowly and ask them to do the same.

Stay with the person in crisis. Do not allow that person to be alone. Remove anything with which he could injure himself. If medical attention is required, call the paramedic or EMT in your area or transport the person to an emergency room. After the medical emergency is resolved, seek a professionally trained counselor. If you don't know of one, call a pastor in your area and ask for a recommendation.

FOR FURTHER THOUGHT

1. As an adolescent yourself, did you ever think of ending your life? Did you consider how you would do it? Did you ever talk to anyone else about such thoughts or ideas? What was their response?

2. Think of a family in which adolescents appear able to communicate with the parents. Do the teenagers appear able to express their emotions, including anger? How do the parents respond? Is there anything to be learned from such a family?

3. Think of a person you know or have read of who attempted suicide. Make a list of your thoughts and feelings toward them. Are you satisfied with your own responses? Write down how you would like to respond to them. How will you make those changes?

4. Consider how teenagers respond to you. Do they appear comfortable being with you? Are you comfortable being with them? Think about conversations with teenagers. Who initiates them? Is there a difference in the flow of conversation depending on who initiates it? What can you learn from past teen-adult communications?

5. Recall your own interests as an adolescent. What did you most enjoy talking and thinking about? What similarities of topics do you observe in teens you know? What differences?

6. Each of us has certain mannerisms or habits that appear peculiar or illogical to others. Subjectively they may be perfectly logical and normal while to others quite unusual. Are you aware of any such behavior of your own? Compare that disparity with that of the teenage suicide attempt. Can you understand how what seems illogical to one can appear logical to another?

And they were bringing children to Him so that He might touch them; and the disciples rebuked them. But when Jesus saw this, He was indignant and said to them, "Permit the children to come to Me; do not hinder them; for the kingdom of God belongs to such as these. . . . And He took them in His arms and began blessing them, laying His hands upon them.

—Mark 10:13–16

There is nothing either good or bad, but thinking makes it so.

—William Shakespeare, *Hamlet*, Act II, Sc. 2

9

THE ATTITUDE OF PREVENTION

THE PYGMALION EFFECT

Several years ago I conducted a workshop for elementary school teachers in a small community outside Charlotte, North Carolina. One of the topics we discussed was the concept of the self-fulfilling prophecy, or the pygmalion effect. This concept has been proved and supported by several independent studies. I will oversimplify the concept for the purposes of this chapter.

The premise of the pygmalion effect in its most basic form is that one's belief will have a major influence on the outcome of an event. The concept was perpetuated in early Greek mythology in the story of Pygmalion. It was later popularized by the fictional professor Henry Higgins and Liza Doolittle in the musical *My Fair Lady*.

In the beginning of the story, Liza is a lowly flower girl, selling flowers on the curbs of London. She flaunts a cockney accent and temperament. Professor Higgins is a rather confident linguist whose only passion is the English language. When he meets Liza, he is insulted by her massacre of the Queen's English. Yet, he believes that by changing the way she speaks, he can pass her off as a duchess at a royal reception.

Liza lacks belief in herself. However, Professor Higgins's own level of confidence is so strong that it has an almost infectious effect. As discouraged as Liza becomes, Professor Higgins is inflappable. He never gives up or expresses resignation around her. Soon his belief in his own abilities convinces Liza that she can eventually pass the test. And she does. His belief is so strong that it influences the outcome of reality.

One of my favorite lines from the play is toward the end. Liza comments that "the difference between a lady and a flower girl is not who she is, it's how she's treated." Treat her like a flower girl, and she will act like a flower girl. But when treated like a lady, she will respond like a lady.

In reality the idea of the self-fulfilling prophecy, or pygmalion, is more complicated than presented by Liza Doolittle. However, her description is eloquent. The belief system we develop about another person will indeed influence the other's behavior. That is true even if we do not verbalize our belief. Somehow, through our behavior, the belief is communicated and does indeed affect others' behavior. In fact, our behavior is far more significant than our words, if there is a discrepancy between the two.

An example of this was demonstrated during experiments in public schools. One researcher convinced teachers that some students (who had actually been chosen at random) had higher IQs than others and would be better performers in the classroom. When the researcher returned many months later, the teachers informed him the chosen students were indeed higher achievers. However, the reality was quite different. Actually the students were no brighter than the others. But somehow the teacher's unverbalized belief had affected the children's performance.

The same effect occurred in a less sterile setting. The same researcher later visited a welding vocational training program. Those in the program included chronically unemployed, recently released convicts, and high school dropouts. He convinced the instructors that a few of the trainees (chosen once again at random) had been found to be "high aptitude personnel." He commented they would be better welders than others in the class. The outcome was identical to the experiment in elementary schools.

The phenomenon of the self-fulfilling prophecy is real. We quite frankly cannot fully explain it. However, we know that it works.

APPLYING PYGMALION

During the workshop I conducted for the elementary school teachers, we investigated the pygmalion effect at great length and practiced utilizing it in the classroom. Several of the teachers approached me after the workshop and shared excitement about applying the concept on the job.

Approximately two years later I received a letter from one of them. She explained her procedure for making "pygmalions" out of her third-graders. She met each one at the door on the first day of class. Bending down on her knees she would whisper, "You must be real smart to get in my class. Only the extra special smart kids get in my grade. Did you know you were that smart?"

She noted that the children's eyes would brighten with wonder at the news. They would exclaim that they "couldn't wait to tell Mom." Her discipline problems decreased, and attendance has improved since implementing that idea. Other teachers began asking what she was doing. Before long they were following the same ritual.

Today that teacher is a school administrator. She was promoted, and the effects of her training of teachers has probably prevented hundreds of cases of adolescent depression and possibly even suicide.

ATTITUDE

Attitude is the real key to prevention of suicide or any other manifestation of depression. The attitude we need to project as parents involves several important facets. The primary one is the sense of expectancy we present toward children. What does our belief system reflect toward them? We can actually build a positive or negative pygmalion.

I try to reflect an attitude different from the radio commentator I mentioned in the previous chapter. My belief about my own children, my young relatives, and the adolescents I work with is quite the opposite. I honestly cannot entertain the attitude that teenagers are uncivilized and depraved.

I think "my kids" are special. They are bright. I like them. They are fun to be with, and I think they are the best generation of young people to ever come along. I believe that. I tell them there is nothing they could do to make me love them any less. And they respond to my belief. I tell them they can do great things with their lives. And they have. I tell them they are brilliant. And they perform brilliantly.

Attitude is perceived by adolescents, and they respond to it. Research and personal experience support the viewpoint that an attitude of positive expectancy will result in positive behavior. The basic core attitude and belief of parents, religious leaders, and educational specialists will set the framework of a child's life. It may be that depression and self-destructive behavior can be prevented merely by a change in the attitude of influential adults or peers.

CONSTRUCTIVE INTERVENTIONS

In 1981 a major urban county reportedly experienced twenty-one adolescent suicides. A plan was implemented in the school district to attempt to impede that trend. Formal discussion groups were designed to talk about issues of adolescent interest. The issues included various topics. Moving, drugs, stress, relationships, or any other subject was allowed. The groups met weekly with a school social worker or counselor. The adult role was simply to be there and facilitate the flow of discussion. The sessions expanded, and other faculty became involved. By 1984 the teen suicide rate in the same county had dropped to zero. When adults expressed their concern by simply being present, suicides were prevented.

I supervised a local high school in implementing a similar program. This was the same school that had experienced two successful suicides and at least six attempts in a three-week period. Suicide attempts have significantly decreased since those support groups were implemented.

A group of this sort accomplishes several major objectives. First, it gives the adolescent at least the opportunity to form a relationship with one significant adult. By making himself available, the adult gives the appearance of caring. The child's belief system then begins to reflect at least one adult who can feel warmth toward that child. It also provides the adolescent with an automatic peer group. Those are teenagers the adolescent's own age who are present for similar reasons. Although it may progress slowly, the comraderie develops and grows. If one group member withdraws, the teens begin to notice and respond. The peer pressure to open up is extremely powerful and far more likely to elicit response than pressure from adults.

Finally, a caring group of this sort gives the teenager a setting where honesty and self-disclosure are encouraged and accepted. A recent newspaper headline read "Confession: Good for More Than the Soul." The article went on to explain that the mere process of talking to someone about troublesome issues had been found to have several positive effects. The most surprising result of the Harvard Medical School study was that it increased the efficiency of the immune system. The immune system is the system within our bodies that helps to prevent diseases and illnesses. The primary consideration is that opening up to another person is an aid to personal health. Thus, I have heard many Roman Catholics claim that going to confession is like "taking a shower." Recent research indicates the process of opening up is even better than a shower. It is an excellent antidote to depression and possibly an aid in suicide prevention.

RAP SESSIONS

Formerly, meetings similar to the one mentioned above were called "rap sessions." In the 1960s rap sessions were very popular. People rapped about various things. Two of the favorite topics were race relations and drug abuse. Often those sessions had no direct leadership. Occasionally, parents would join their children to rap. It appears that this particular level of involvement was probably a good way to stay in touch with teens. The same thing would work for parents today.

It is equally important for teens to respond to each

other. Adolescents are simply more honest among themselves than they usually are with their parents. We cannot truly enter the world of our children. It is essentially cut off from our experience. However, we can approach and touch it. Teens, being in the same world, have greater opportunity to detect difficulty within each other. Making adolescents aware of the crisis of suicide is probably one way to prevent its spreading.

FAMILY GROUPS

In the early 1970s I was involved in an experimental project involving multiple family group therapy sessions. The bi-weekly sessions included combined families. The purpose of the group evolved around an addicted adolescent member who was referred by the local courts. It was an interesting program.

Because of the inclusiveness of family members, there was little opportunity for the adolescent to be dishonest or ignore the problem. It was equally impossible for parents to deny their responsibility to the adolescent. The growth and development expressed by those who attended was phenomenal. Watching the members develop by confronting different issues was similar to participating in an evolving human drama. The most rewarding part of the experiment was to watch families heal each other. In my years of professional experience since that time I can recall nothing quite as rewarding. On the other hand I also do not recall anything as exhausting for the therapist.

ASSERTIVENESS AND PREVENTIVE EXPRESSION

One psychologist describes depression as the inability to behave in a way that would evoke stimulating and pleasurable reactions from others. By functioning as part of a group such as has been described, an adolescent can learn from peers and significant adults behavior that will result in favorable responses. Some people also recommend assertiveness training for depressed adolescents. Modeling assertive behavior is quickly learned by adolescents. As they receive favorable response for becoming more outspoken, their own assertiveness is reinforced.

A teenager is less likely to remain depressed as he or she gains greater verbal or behavioral self-assurance. In that sense expression is the opposite of depression, and it is reflected by attitude following behavior. If a person acts depressed, he eventually will feel depressed. If he acts enthusiastically, then the attitude of enthusiasm will follow.

As a young athlete I often did not feel like going to practice or attending training sessions. However, the sense of obligation was so great that I would attend anyway. Once I became involved in the activity it was enjoyable, and I "felt" like continuing.

Behavior, in this way, often precedes attitude. Thus, one of the values of group activity for adolescents is establishing a sense of obligation toward group members to "be" or "act" in a healthy manner as expected by fellow group members.

SUPPORT SYSTEMS

Many people rely on various forms of support groups. Those groups can be professional organizations, Sunday school classes, or just informal gatherings of friends. A support group can take almost any form. Regardless of form, the composition is one of people who are supportive and encouraging to each other.

Such a network can be an invaluable asset. Some groups are formal and structured. Others are less formal but nonetheless supportive. Adults also need support groups. They can be found or created anywhere. They do not require a trained counselor as leader, since their purpose is not counseling but support. The interest and caring of others that grows from such a core unit can help prevent emotional distress.

An adolescent without a support group is in trouble. If an adolescent makes or receives no telephone calls, that is one sign that the adolescent may have no system of support. If an adolescent never invites friends home or receives no invitations to go home with others, that may be another signal. Some children need encouragement and assistance in forming peer relationships. Occasionally parents have to aid the teenager in finding a group of people with whom he or she can feel comfortable.

One readily available place to find a potential support group is a church. There the adolescent can usually find people his own age and adults who indeed care. Occasionally a child may not feel comfortable with a particular group of adolescents at a church. It may be necessary then to consider changing churches. It is much easier for an adult to adapt than for an adolescent. The teenager's interests need to be considered more than the adult's at this critical stage of development.

Naturally, some inquiry will help determine the reason for the youth's lack of comfort. If the adolescent is simply shy and withdrawn, changing churches is not the only solution. However, it is fairly common for an adolescent who feels left out or alienated from one group to be able to blend and fit in well with another. I have seen dozens of such examples in the past few years. There is a wide enough variety of youth groups available today to expect a fit for any adolescent's personality.

THE CHURCH'S RESPONSIBILITY

Churches have a long history of working with teenagers to meet their social and emotional needs. The opportunity for helping teenagers today is greater than ever before. The challenge is also greater. Today's adolescents are exposed to far more information and technology than most adults can even imagine. Simply holding their attention can be a major accomplishment. However, teens do respond if adults express a personal interest in them as people.

The story of "Bear" is one good example. Bear is actually a youth minister of a church in Georgia.

When Bear began his ministry at the church he found the youth program with a very small membership. He placed his newly framed doctorate on the wall and decided to begin Bible studies. According to Bear, his attitude was, "Here I am, kids; I'm ready to teach you. Come and get it."

Nobody came.

After a few weeks of review and contemplation, he decided to change his approach. He grew a beard, removed his tie, took his degree from the wall, and became "Bear." The youth program eventually soared and has mushroomed to touch a majority of the adolescents in the area.

Bear's approach sought to reach children where they live. Bear indicated that he chose to meet the needs of the children and get their attention. Since rapport was thus established, they are much more receptive when he approaches them for study. One teenager put it this way: "Act like you are interested in giving me a Bible study, and I may or may not listen. But act like you are interested in me, and I will return."

Bear suggests the focus of youth work is one of "sowing and not necessarily reaping." He refers to adolescence as a "twilight zone," during which the teenager needs a relationship to keep him in touch with reality. When parents lose sight of their own adolescent years, problems are increased. Bear sees his work as relational.

That particular point of view was supported in a survey of former National Merit Scholars. Those erstwhile scholarship winners were asked to rate characteristics of successful teachers. Without exception the leading quality was that of a relational nature. The scholars listed the most important quality as "expressing a close personal interest in me as a person." Knowledge of subject area was far down the list of important qualities.

Churches would be the primary target of support for adolescents. A church has all the elements to provide encouragement and hope for today's teens. When properly presented there can be no hope greater than the love of God expressed in Jesus Christ. However, when improperly presented, an adolescent will either lose interest or totally reject the church's potential stability.

LEARNING THE LANGUAGE

It is a known fact that Americans are more widely accepted by people in other countries if they learn the language of the country they are visiting. Even though our attempts may be sophomoric, the native-speaking countrymen appreciate the gesture. Obvious language barriers exist if we attempt communicating to those people in a different language than they speak.

The same point must be considered with today's adolescents. They speak a different language. They live in a different culture. We need to approach them on a level that will gain and hold their attention. Today's teens have been weaned on a fast-paced track. Watching an episode of Sesame Street illustrates that pace.

The skits are brief. Each lasts only seconds. There is prolific color and movement. Voices are animated and varied. Locations change drastically. Music abounds. There is quick but clear and precise dialogue. If there is a slow-moving conversation, as an example between Big Bird and Snuffleupagus, it is quickly followed by an upbeat song with marching or movement. The pace is incredibly rapid and varied. And the show is successful.

Probably most of today's adolescents do not watch Sesame Street. However, many of them grew up on it. The show also represents the quality of television programming today's adolescents have been exposed to. It is just one good example of the extremes to which we must go to capture and hold their attention. The competition for teens' time and attention is fierce. That does not mean we need to dilute or weaken what is said. It just means that communicating requires a language they will hear.

Ron Hutchcraft, heard on the Moody Broadcasting Network, has achieved this better than anyone I have heard. His radio program "Saturday Night Alive" is an excellent example and has an extremely successful formula. The program is fast-paced, varied, and colorful, with upbeat music interspersed with phone calls and discussion among teens. He obviously has some strong information to communicate. It does not sound diluted, yet teenagers listen and respond. His program is a good learning ground for adults to also listen and hear how Ron accomplishes what he does.

By approaching teens in a way to which they will listen, we are preventing many of the emotional crises that can lead to severe problems.

"HELPING" AND PREVENTION

Certain behaviors may reinforce suicidal gestures. These responses are often intended as "helping." Occasionally, however, they can actually strengthen the possibility of subsequent suicide attempts.

Parents need to insure that attention is paid to adolescents when they are not acting out or behaving in self-destructive fashion. Attention strengthens behavior. Therefore, one way to increase healthy responses is to reward them with attention. If the only time a teenager has a lengthy discussion with a parent is in crisis periods, there are likely to be more crises. If a teenaged girl can only get attention from men by flirting, she is more likely to flirt. Basically, an adolescent will do whatever is necessary to get attention from others. If the teenager is given sufficient positive attention for proper and appropriate behavior, usually positive behavior will continue.

Occasionally, a teenager may need counseling by a professional. A counselor or psychotherapist must be able to form a relationship with the adolescent that revolves around more than the problem. If the counselor is purely problem-oriented with an adolescent, the problematic behavior is going to be reinforced. Equally important, if the counselor is only problem oriented, the teenager will probably refuse to attend the sessions. Parents need to understand that cultivating a relationship of trust takes a great deal of time and attention and will only occur over a span of time. That is true in any relationship but even more so in the counseling setting.

Counseling accomplished properly will not reinforce problem behavior. The sessions will eventually need to focus on tension-reducing behavior and alternatives to problems. However, getting to that point will not occur immediately.

In a few cases medication may be required for effective counseling treatment. If that occurs, it is best in most instances that the adolescent is involved in counseling sessions during the entire period of drug administration. If the teenager takes medication without counseling, there may be a danger of reinforcing a drug-seeking approach to problem-solving. In any case, it is best to consult a child psychiatrist if medication is needed.

The chosen counselor may be a psychiatrist, psychologist, marriage and family counselor, or other trained professional. Most pastors are also trained in counseling and can give spiritual perspective. The important thing is to seek their services in the event of a crisis of very blatant adolescent depression or feared suicide attempts. Prevention is the key word.

Develop an attitude of unconditional positive regard for the child. Let him think there is nothing he can do to make you love him less. Take seriously every threat, comment, or behavior that appears to be self-destructive or depressive. Treating a gesture of that nature lightly is sending the wrong signal to the teen.

A sincere and immediate expression of caring concern is the best response. Rather than disagreeing or trying to rationalize the teenager's comment, listen noncritically to what he has to say. Ask the teenager straightforwardly if he is considering suicide. Whatever the response, express concern and love. Remove any object with which the adolescent could injure himself. Then seek professional help.

Most important, develop a close relationship with your own and other adolescents. That has proved to be one of the primary tools in suicide prevention. Compassion and love have an unbelievable effect on teenagers.

Direct some of that compassion toward your own teenager's friends. They are the best source of accurate information about your child's emotional well-being. If you sincerely befriend them, they will let you know if your own child is in trouble. It does not take a great deal of time or attention. But the small investment can reap big rewards.

FOR FURTHER THOUGHT

1. How would you rate your own attitude toward the teens in your life? On a scale of 1–10 (1 = very negative/ 10 = very positive), what is your general expectancy of them? Are there certain topics or issues on which you have difficulty expressing a positive verbal or nonverbal attitude?

2. With regard to those "touchy" issues, do your verbal and nonverbal attitudes match, or do you experience conflict between what you say and feel?

3. Are there any teens in your life that you consider "safe" from suicide? Stop a moment and consider why. Keep in mind that achievements and other outward signs of success may be deceiving. Have you convinced yourself that, in fact, no one is immune from the possibility of suicide?

4. How prepared are you to deal with a teenager in genuine life-threatening distress? How willing are you? Do you expose yourself to elements of the teen world in order to understand and speak their language?

5. As a potential "life saver," review the social network of the teens in your life. What areas are strong forces? Which ones are weak? How can you strengthen their social network?

For as he thinketh in his heart, so is he.

—Proverbs 23:7, KJV

As the plant springs from and could not be, without the seed, so every act of a man springs from the hidden seeds of thought. And could not have appeared without them.

—James Lane Allen

10

THE SELF-ESTEEM
CONNECTION

It has been suggested by many authorities that one of the best ways to prevent emotional problems among adolescents is to help them achieve high self-esteem. That is an easy statement to make and a difficult process to master.

TABULA RASA

Aristotle stated that our personality at birth is like a blank slate or tablet, a tabula rasa. It is blank until experience writes on it, and thus personality and self-esteem are originated.

Modern researchers do not completely agree with Aristotle, but there are certain elements of truth in his hypothesis. Personality is based somewhat on the input of personal experience. Charles Horton Cooley built a theory of personality on the Aristotelian concept of tabula rasa.

He suggested that each of us effectively look into a mirror held up to us by society. We observe how others respond to us and make certain basic decisions about our self-worth and individual self-esteem. Therefore, when I look out into society I am not only looking at the members but also observing specifically how they respond to me.

If that response is positive, then I feel positive about who and what I am. If the response is negative, then I am less satisfied about my own sense of self. In that way society provides me with a looking glass that influences my self-esteem. Certainly, personality development is quite more complex than Aristotle and Cooley suggested. A variety of factors influence the individual. Obviously, biochemical changes affect personality and behavior. Yet, to a degree, both Cooley and Aristotle gave us valuable insight.

In some ways we are like a computer. Or perhaps it would be more accurate to say in some ways a computer resembles us. The modern acronym *GIGO* applies here: garbage in, garbage out. If the only input we receive is negative, then we will be affected with a negative outlook on life. And just as negativism is contagious, so is enthusiasm.

Many years ago I attended a Toastmasters Club outside Charlotte, North Carolina. For those unfamiliar with Toastmasters, it has nothing to do with toasting or drinking. Toastmasters is an educational organization devoted to helping people become better public speakers. (Incidentally, I have recommended literally hundreds of people to Toastmasters, both adolescents and adults, as one way to build positive self-esteem.)

This particular club met at 7:00 A.M. on Saturday mornings. Members included people of all races and positions in life. The one thing those people had in common was a contagious enthusiasm. I always walked away from the meetings much more energized than when I walked in. I liked myself better when I left and felt like helping others. It was because of the input and enthusiasm I received from the Toastmasters Club. Handshakes, applause, backslapping, and encouragement were dished out in abundant helpings. The support and enthusiasm was contagious and had an impact on my self-esteem. Instead of garbage going in, I exposed myself to enthusiasm going in. As a result, I felt better, and my output was enthusiasm.

A CASE OF GIGO

Dan had made an appointment with me at the encouragement of his father. He was an olive-skinned, dark-eyed late adolescent. The baggy circles beneath his eyes made him appear older than his relatively few years. His eyes twitched occasionally as he spoke. There seemed to be a constant movement about him. It was not a fluid movement, but more of an arrhythmic jerk.

"I don't know. I just came here because my father wanted me to," Dan responded to me uncomfortably.

"What did your dad think you needed to work on?"

"I guess he thinks something is wrong with me. I don't want to go to medical school like he wants me to. He thinks I am depressed or something."

"Do you think you are depressed?"

"I guess. I don't know. I haven't felt all that great lately. The only thing I really care about is my music."

"Tell me about your music. What do you listen to?"

Dan visibly lightened. His body shifted forward, and he made eye contact with me for the first time.

"Oh, you have never heard of it probably. Did you ever listen to 'underground'?"

"I don't think so." I could only shrug.

"You remember Sid Vicious?"

"Yes. I thought he had died."

Dan grew more animated as I at least could identify that I was not totally ignorant in his eyes.

"Well, yeah, but I like his music. Did you really ever listen to him?"

"Actually I didn't listen to the music. It seems I've seen something about him on TV."

Dan's gaze lowered. "I don't ever watch TV," he responded. "It's a sellout. Too commercial. I mean it's just like what you hear on the radio. Those people just write music to make money. It's just too commercial."

There were a few seconds of silence.

"So what do you listen to? What's 'underground'?"

"Well, it's just real low-down music. You can't get it here—nobody sells it. I order it through the mail."

"Is it rock?" I still wasn't sure what he was referring to.

"Sort of. It's real down. One guy killed himself after cutting an album. I mean the stuff he sang was depressing. He cut the album and then committed suicide within an hour. Sold a lot of tapes though."

"Serious?" I wasn't sure.

"Yeah. He did it. Pretty cool, huh?"

We continued our conversation, and I began to share the concern of Dan's father. This adolescent was listening to "his music" literally eighteen to twenty-one hours per day. He listened on headphones at work. He listened in his car. He even listened to it in his sleep, which, in my opinion, was far more dangerous than when he was awake. Dan had several problems. Besides the music, he was using a wide variety of drugs. He needed to be detoxified both from the drugs and the music. Neither his father nor I were initially successful at getting Dan to reverse his lifestyle. He actually needed to be treated in a hospital or rehabilitation center. Yet he persistently refused that option.

Several months after our initial visit, Dan was injured in an automobile accident. He spent six days in the hospital. During that time he was without drugs or music. Upon discharge he checked himself into a drug treatment center and began a very slow and painful recovery process. He continues to improve, as does his self-esteem. His was a case in which the powerful negative "garbage in" was resulting in serious "garbage out" thinking and beliefs. Fortunately, it was reversed.

OUTPUT EQUALS INPUT

Dan was like a robot. He was soaking up the constant instructional programming of the music, drugs, and lifestyle. It was reflected in his personality. We all operate on the same principle.

Some years ago I attended a weekend training conference for helping professions: psychiatrists, psychologists, marriage and family counselors, and social workers. As in many of the training programs I attend, it was a show-and-tell conference. The presenters talked about their philosophy of treatment and then illustrated it by offering demonstration sessions to those in attendance. Of the forty who attended the conference, ten volunteered for demonstrations.

Those ten ranged in age from mid 30s to early 60s. Three were adult children of former physicians, and one was the adult child of a rabbi. Of those ten, nine people chose to work on issues surrounding their relationship with their parents. The issue in all nine cases could be summarized as lack of time.

When I returned from the conference I told my wife—no matter how busy I ever became—never to allow me to ignore our children. She has been quite cooperative, as she also recognizes the powerful impact that positive time with parents can have on self-esteem.

QUALITY INPUT

Because of the nature of my profession I often work evenings. When I return home on those evenings, the children are sometimes asleep. On those occasions I individually pick them up, sit in the rocking chair, and begin rocking slowly. I start a monolog telling them about my feelings.

"You know, I love you very much. You're probably the most wonderful creature God has ever produced. You are smart and kind, and you are a very nice boy. I think you are great. Daddy loves you, Momma loves you, and the whole world loves you."

They sometimes respond. Usually it's just a grunt. The oldest one sometimes says, "Yea!"

He knows it. He's heard it all before. We give them similar messages when they are awake. But actually, that kind of input is probably more powerful if given sometime either right before they are asleep or else during the first ninety minutes of rest.

I have terrific children, and they have high self-esteem. I think one of the reasons is this sort of input, or programming.

SELF-CONCEPT IN LATE ADOLESCENCE

For most adolescents, self-concept does not come from within. It comes from group identification. During late adolescence that process begins to change. But a transition is not complete until early adulthood.

For a teenager, identity is not a product of who he is. Instead it originates from what he does. Self-esteem comes from being on the football team, or playing in the band, or driving a particular car. It is important for parents to realize this and help their teenagers and younger children to begin to develop something from which they can gain a unique identity. As adults, we realize that true self-esteem comes from within rather than outside of a person. Yet, that is developmentally almost impossible for an adolescent. We must utilize what the adolescent is capable of experiencing at any particular moment. We can encourage that young person for just "being" as well as for any accomplishments.

A CASE OF SELF-ESTEEM DEVELOPMENT

Several years ago I was preparing to go on a week-long skiing trip. A few of my friends were giving me some good-natured ribbing.

"Don't you come back here with a broken arm, looking for sympathy," I was told enviously. "You won't get any!"

"Oh, I wouldn't do that," I replied. "I like myself too much to break an arm."

Later, I chuckled about the teasing. But as I thought about it more, I realized something of significance. I actually did like myself too much to be careless and break an arm. And I did not have to be doing anything to like myself. Just "being" was enough.

In high school I liked myself because I played football, or received all-state honors, or dated a certain girl. Later, it was because I was a marine, or a paratrooper, or a marathoner. My self-esteem was because of what I did, not who I was. Now, after many years I finally liked myself because I was John.

It was a developmental step toward self-esteem.

THE MIDDLE CHILD

Working with the Ames family was a pleasure. The parents and children loved and respected each other. The father was an anchorman for a California television newscast and popular in the community. The mother was a cosmetics consultant and had been rewarded for her sales and recruitment. The eldest son was a handsome young man who had been the starting quarterback on the high school football team since his sophomore year. He had already been offered scholarships by several major colleges. The youngest child, Sarah, was beautiful. She was one of those young people who sparkle with warmth. At age fourteen she had already earned over $10,000 modeling for local stores and magazines.

And then there was the middle child. Oh, yes. What's his name? Jeff's little brother, you know. Sarah's older brother. Not Jeff, but the other one.

There was nothing wrong with John. He simply had been surpassed in popularity by the others. They were all tough acts to follow. Actually, he was doing OK in his own right. He simply had no unique identity. He was still "the other kid." John didn't play football, model, sell cosmetics, or anchor the news. In fact, there was no unique skill at which he excelled. He was successful at everything he attempted; however, he specialized in no one area. It was essential to find a niche for John.

We went through a variety of activities. John tried them all with enthusiasm. Scuba diving was fun, but there was little opportunity for competition, and he wanted to compete. One day he was looking around my office and saw a picture of some bicycle racers. It held his interest for more than a few brief silent moments.

"Do you race bikes?" he asked.

"No. Not now. I used to." I gazed at the picture along with him.

"Is it hard?"

"Well, it sure can be. You have to work up to it. But you can get involved on all levels. I think you'd like to try it?"

He waited before answering.

"Do you get to wear a uniform?" He gazed at me earnestly.

"Yes," I responded with an attempt at sincerity. "And a number!"

Shortly afterwards, John's parents purchased him a professional racing bike and the appropriate jersey, shorts, and shoes. John joined a southern California bicycle club. Several months later he began racing. Within a year he became competitive.

Today, John is a college student in northern California

and still races. But more important, his self-esteem soared. It blasted off when he began developing a unique identity.

Bicycle racing is obviously not the issue. The bicycle was only an important avenue to self-esteem development. With some adolescents you have to expend a great deal of energy and utilize a wide variety of resources. It is important in those cases to understand the various agents of socialization.

AGENTS OF SOCIALIZATION

Self-esteem can be influenced by a number of resources. All of these fall within one of five general categories. The more quality parents can assure from these agents of socialization, the higher self-esteem will be.

FAMILY

The family is a primary source of influence, especially during the first six to ten years of the child's life. This naturally changes as the child grows older. However, virtually all experts agree that the first five years are the most important in core personality development.

The importance and significance of love, compassion, and an unconditional positive regard cannot be overemphasized. As parents, we are setting the foundation in the home throughout our children's lives. Even after the child leaves, or the primary influential force in socialization changes, the family remains significant.

SCHOOL

Obviously teachers have more time with children beyond the age of six than most parents. Their influence is extremely important to the personality development and belief system of the child.

The debate currently exists and will persist concerning the value of public versus private education. I am more concerned about the quality of caring exhibited by the teacher than where he or she teaches. The nature of the student-teacher relationship is going to be of much more importance to the child than where the child attends school.

Parents need to be aware of the kind of input our children are receiving from this very critical relationship.

PEERS

It is difficult to control whom adolescents choose for their friends. It is also dangerous to try to pick their associates. We are tempted to do that occasionally, and sometimes it may work, but any such attempt may backfire. The adolescent may then unconsciously seek those we wish they wouldn't. Such reactions by children are predictable, and may be essential as adolescents rapidly move toward greater autonomy and self-responsibility.

It is likely that our children will choose their friends from the most easily accessible group. The issue then becomes whom we make accessible through school, neighborhoods, churches, and social organizations. Thus, our primary target for input in choice of friends is indirect but important.

MEDIA

The influence of media has been briefly discussed earlier. It is incredibly powerful and impossible to ignore. A wise choice might be to utilize the media to the child's advantage. Utilization is the important consideration.

It is important to be accessible and observe what adolescents are learning from the media. Watch what they are absorbing on television. Observe your child's response to the program. Consider movies your adolescents ask to see. What is it about the movie that interests them? Ratings are sometimes not appropriate measures. I have screened G-rated movies that could have been extremely destructive to a child. Parents should exercise their own evaluation, keeping in mind the value and belief systems to which the adolescent will be exposed.

It is also useful to read the newspaper and see what movies teen are viewing. Through the newspaper we can also learn about the albums they are buying and the concerts they are attending. Basically, let the media inform you about the values to which your teen is being exposed. Otherwise parents will be insulated and lost. That could result in a true communication gap.

CHURCH

Church is the final agent of socialization. It is listed last because on the average it has the least quantity of influence on adolescent socialization. The truth is, the church has all the necessary resources to fill gaps in modern American society. The fact that some say it is failing to do so is probably due in part to the fault of the church for not being more responsive, and because parents do not participate more actively.

Each of those socialization agents has an impact on self-esteem. The more positive input received from each, the more enriched a child's resources will become. The genetic predisposition to a certain temperament may be constant to some degree. However, other influences can be manipulated. These influences are found in the agents of socialization. In many ways they are avenues to self-esteem development.

Encouraging Goals

I am really not sure how high the tower was at the lake. There were four levels, beginning about three feet above the water. Adults could stand and walk between each level, so I assume they were a minimum of seven feet apart. That would have made the fourth level a minimum of twenty-five feet above the water.

In June I had told my father I wanted to dive from the top level before summer ended. That was a high dive and a high goal for an eight-year-old. But I decided I wanted to do it.

Most of the summer I just stared at the tower. Occasionally I would jump off the third level. I once climbed up on the fourth level, looked down cautiously, and slinked back down two levels. It was intimidating! In August, Dad accompanied me to the lake. He had told me this would probably be the last time we could go. No mention was made of the dive.

My sister and I went in separate directions as usual. After she left, Dad came walking over.

"You know, you said you wanted to go off the high tower. This is it. Probably your last chance."

"Yes—it's pretty high." I looked up. To my little eight-year-old eyes, it rivaled the Empire State Building.

"Well, I know, but you said you wanted to. Look, you're my boy whether you dive or not. But just in case you want to go through with it, here is the best way." He then went through a complete explanation of how the dive would be made, beginning with climbing up the ladder. After the explanation, he demonstrated fully by climbing up the tower himself and making the dive. He even gave a Tarzan yell from the top! I met him at the beach after he swam back and told him what a good dive it was.

"Well, it was OK. Doing it is the main thing. Anybody can tell you about diving. Doing it, even if it's sloppy, is what's important. By the way, the Tarzan yell was extra."

I thought silently for a moment.

He spoke again.

"Well, I guess you had better go ahead and get wet. We can only stay for a little while. Have fun! And by the way—" he made eye contact with me "—don't forget the Tarzan yell."

It was my goal. Not his. I could only go ahead and do it. After all, I couldn't make a Tarzan yell if I didn't dive! I'm sure my father realized that fact.

It was just the way he had described it. I climbed up the ladder slowly, conserving my energy. It was almost as if I was on remote control. I didn't even notice the second or third level. As I reached the top, I walked to the edge, leaned over, continued walking, and made my dive.

I forgot the Tarzan yell on top so I made it on the way down and even had time to laugh. My dad was more elated than I was on my return. He picked me up and bragged on the dive. He repeated the story to others for several weeks.

I had set my own goal. But I needed encouragement from him. It is still that way for me. Adults need encouragement. But for an adolescent, encouragement is absolutely vital.

Goals, whether made alone or with parental help, are constructive for adolescents. They are more than just guideposts to help in direction. A goal-setting session with a teenager will help him get perspective on where he is going. It will also give the child some idea of what he can accomplish. Parental encouragement as children approach and attain goals will bring the family closer together.

I practice this system with adolescents as well as my own family. It has been exceptionally rewarding. Goals add hope and encourage persistence that helps build self-esteem. A word of special note is that we need to let our teens know we love them regardless of their achievement level. Whether they succeed or fail at goal attainment, they must be assured of our emotional commitment. We love them for who they are, not what they do. That promise gives them hope and courage to try without fear of failure.

The more specific a goal, the better. My goal was to jump off the fourth level before summer was over. The task (jump off the tower) was behaviorally oriented and observable. I would know if I completed it. It involved the behavior of jumping. Therefore it was reasonably objective. A time measurement was attached. I wanted to achieve it by a certain date. The task was progressive. I could make logical sequential steps toward completing the objective. I could start with the first level and work up to the fourth in graduated steps.

As I progressed toward achieving the goal, I was rewarded at each step. The ultimate reward came on jumping from the top level. My self-esteem rose higher than the four levels from which I jumped.

Encouraging goal-setting and goal-achievement among teenagers is a rewarding way to build self-esteem.

DELAYED GRATIFICATION

The ability to delay gratification is one that results not only in some degree of maturity, but also in high self-esteem. This ability is one that does not come easily. As babies we cried when we were wet and expected to get changed. We cried when we were hungry and expected to be fed. However, as we become more sophisticated it is hoped that we develop the ability to delay immediate gratification. It is sacrificed for gratification of a higher nature at some later date. The ability to delay gratification is essential in the lives of most adults. The unwillingness to develop that skill can be a big factor in adolescent and adult depression.

A CASE OF DELAYED GRATIFICATION

By age fifteen my life had changed substantially. Mother had remarried after my father's death. We had moved to the mountains of western North Carolina and lived on my step-father's farm. I had adapted as quickly as one could to the new life-style. Although my chores were demanding, especially for a young adolescent, it was a great life. During the fall of my sophomore year in high school, however, things began to change.

I was a starting offensive lineman on the football team, and the only sophomore to bear that distinction. Even though I was big for my age, I wasn't as strong as some of the older boys. As a result I occasionally got roughed up during practice and came home exhausted. After several weeks of this I talked to my step-father about the chores. I wondered if we could change them until after football season. He said no; I had agreed to what they would be and would have to continue. That presented a problem. I could not drive and had to hitchhike home. To catch the school bus in the morning, I had to first do all my morning chores. That necessitated getting up at 5:00 A.M. The evening chores, including milking the cows, had to be completed before I could rest or do homework. My day lasted from 5:00 A.M. until 11:00 P.M., without a break.

I complained and whined to my mother and step-father until finally they relented. I probably brought unfair pressure into the situation by complaining so much. But I got my way and felt good about that.

A week or two later my mother suggested we talk.

"I think you may have won the battle, but you're losing the war."

"What?" I had no idea what my mother was trying to say.

She looked at me for a moment and then responded gently.

"You have won the battle, but you're losing the war."

"Are you talking about football? What do you mean?" She certainly had my attention.

"No. With your step-father. You have won the battle. You don't have to do your work. But you are going to lose in the long run. I really think you need to just go ahead and start doing your chores again."

"No. Uh-uh. Nope, I'm not going to do that. I never even get to sleep anymore. Just wait till after football season."

"Son, that will be December. He'd have to pay somebody else double what he pays you. You're very important around here. He bought those new heifers because you were able to take care of them."

"I'm not going to do that. It's not fair. Let Sonia do them."

"She can't. She doesn't know anything about your jobs. Besides, she has her own work to do." She paused for a few moments and then asked, "Son, have I ever lied to you?"

"I don't know," I waited. "I don't think so."

"Do you trust me?"

"Yeah, sure." I knew I was losing.

"Believe me, son, go ahead and do them. You will be glad before it's over with. Do it for me."

I did. To save time, I refined my system for doing everything. It really wasn't all that bad. Winter passed quickly, then spring. In April I turned sixteen. Happy day!

"John, son, I need to talk to you." It was my step-father.

"Sure." I wondered what I had done 'wrong.

"Son, I have been wanting to talk to you. You're sixteen now, and, well, you have been an awful lot of help to me around here. Really, you've never been much trouble. I'll tell you what, why don't you just drive that old Cadillac like it's yours. It's not the best car, but it will get you around. That way you won't have to get up quite so early in the morning."

I remember literally jumping up and down. I had no idea I was going to get to drive the Cadillac. I had only gotten my driver's license a few days earlier. I hugged my step-father and my mother and ran outside. I spent an hour in the car without moving it. It was great! By learning to delay gratification, my self-esteem and I both got a lift.

Mother was right. I put in my time and got the reward. My step-father was the best "country psychologist" I have ever met. Immediate gratification would have been to avoid doing the chores I had been asked to do to sleep longer in the morning. Learning the principle of delayed gratification was much more important to my self-esteem than getting the car, although the car helped!

FOR FURTHER THOUGHT

1. Remember your teenage years and list significant persons and values you learned from each of the agents of socialization. What was the single most important factor influencing your self-esteem?

2. Consider the source of your self-esteem today. Is it influenced more from within or without? In what way or ways? What parallels or contrasts do you observe in your self-esteem level and your moods?

3. Assess your skills of goal-setting and ability to delay gratification on a scale of 1–10 (1=low skill/10=high skill). Have you achieved the mastery level you desire? If not, what will you do to change?

4. Think of a teenager you know well. Consider the influence you have on that person. In which category of agents of socialization do you have the greatest impact on this teen? What are you actively doing to influence that person?

5. Think of all the teens you know. Does any one particularly strike you as in need of more quality input? What can you do to help? Will you?

See that you do not despise one of these little ones, for I say to you, that their angels in heaven continually behold the face of my Father who is in heaven. Thus it is not the will of your Father who is in heaven that one of these little ones perish.

—Matthew 18:10, 14

The domestic affections are the principal source of human happiness and well-being. The mutual loves of husband and wife, of parents and children, of brothers and sisters, are not only the chief sources of happiness, but the chief springs of action, and the chief safeguards from evil.

—Charles W. Eliot

11

TUNING IN TO ADOLESCENTS

ELEMENTS OF FINE TUNING

Many parents today are disturbed as they observe their teens literally "tuned in to" music videos. At times the videos seem to absorb the youngsters. They sit with eyes glued to the screen. Their bodies respond and seem to merge with the music.

In a similar way, we parents need to become absorbed with our adolescents. That means unstopping our sensory channels and not only observing but responding to the adolescent's life stages. Ingredients needed to accomplish that are equal measures of time, concentration, and love. One of those characteristics alone is insufficient. All elements must be present to understand and be of assistance to adolescents today. Throughout this book thus far, various influences on adolescent depression and suicide have been investigated. In this chapter some of the key elements of "tuning in to adolescents" will be discussed.

TUNING IN TO PARENT/CHILD RELATIONSHIPS

I met Sam in marriage counseling. I had never worked with anyone else from a similar background. His parents

had both been in the film industry and were extremely
wealthy. Sam had grown up in a mansion. As a child he
had his own staff of butlers, valets, and governesses. At
one time his parents had even hired playmates to be company for Sam.

Because of filming schedules his parents were seldom
around during Sam's childhood. When they were, there
was little individual time to spend with him. Sam clearly
resembled his father. He was often paraded out in public
so others could see the similarities. His father appeared
proud of him, yet there was simply no relationship. Over
the years Sam became bitter because of a genuine void he
felt.

He was now an adult. He lived with his wife and their
children. There had been multiple separations and near
divorces during this relationship. In fact, it was Sam's third
marriage. The major presenting complaint was his lack of
patience with children. In dealing with them, he had virtually no control over his temper. When things became tense
he would yell and threaten them. Sometimes he broke
valuable items during angry rages. He was exceptionally
demanding.

We spent a great deal of time in family counseling. At
one point that even included Sam's parents, as well as his
wife's. There seemed to be no role model for an effective
father. Sam was extremely good at being overly protective
and ingratiating. His governness had been an excellent
role model for those characteristics. However, when tension or frustration arose, he simply had no idea how to
respond.

Sam had never seen his parents disagree. In fact, he had
seldom seen them at all. When reciting childhood memo-
ries he would tell of the few interactions he recalled. Most
of those centered around spankings and angry confrontations between him and his mother. With his own children,
Sam was being the best parent he could. His behavior was
a reproduction of what he had learned. At one point, he
reflected on his relationship with his parents.

"What I really needed was a good kick in the pants," he
commented.

"No, you're wrong," I answered. "What you really needed was a relationship with your parents."

Sam never understood. As a child the little interaction he had had from his parents was negative. The predominant emotion he had come to associate with being a parent was anger. In his subconsious mind he had equated parental attention with spankings and yelling. So that is what he did as a parent. Sam's parents never tuned in to him, and he didn't know how to tune in to his children.

Predictably, Sam dropped out of counseling when it became apparent that we would have to work at developing certain characteristics. He had never learned to do that either.

TUNING IN TO TIME

A positive relationship with adolescents must be composed of quantity as well as quality time. That requires opportunity for the relationship to be groomed and nurtured. Time must be spent with the teenager exclusively, in circumstances other than disciplinary situations.

I often urge fathers and mothers to set aside one night per week or every other week for each individual child. On that night I encourage the father to take the teenager out away from the home and provide time and substance for the relationship to grow. Teenagers need to have the security of a strong relationship with parents. Without such to rely on, there is no foundation on which to build further emotional growth. Spending this time with teens closes generation gaps and allows for further tuning into them.

THE IMPORTANCE OF RELATIONSHIPS

Early psychological theorists indicated that suicide was an aggressive impulse that resulted from anger over the loss of a love object. The loss could be real or imagined. Others suggested that depression originated from anger turned inward.

Carl Menninger later supported that assertion in his discussion of suicide. Menninger expanded on these ideas, however, and submitted that the loss could also include loss of self-esteem or some other ideal.

Dealing with loss is one of the most painful and complicated processes to accomplish, even under the best of
circumstances. But it is exceptionally true when there is a
sparse social network available from which to draw strength.
It is also important to point out that loss can include a
number of things, not just a person or relationship.

There are reported cases of depression among adolescents following broken romances or the loss of a close
friend. Such relationship dissolutions are much more traumatic for those adolescents who have been deprived of
other meaningful relationships. However, some experts
state that it is not the loss of the relationship that causes
the suicide attempt. Rather, it is caused instead by what the
adolescent experiences as a loss of love itself. Or, in the
adolescent's mind, what he sees as the loss of hope.

Clearly this love and hope can come from healthy relationships. Emphasis was made earlier on the importance of
peer and significant adult relationships. Tuning in to adolescents means we do whatever is necessary to assure opportunities are presented for our teens to develop these
relationships.

After my father passed away in my own childhood, I
developed a more intense relationship with my grandfather. Later I developed several relationships with different
adults, who opened their homes and lives to me. My step-
father died shortly after my sixteenth birthday. That loss
was more devastating than when my father died. It brought
back unconscious feelings I had of being rejected by my
father at his death. When I grieved my stepfather's death,
I unconsciously relived my father's death as well.

I was fortunate in that there was a cadre of loving and
caring adults in my community who took over. The pastor
of our church at that time was the first to respond. Then
our director of Christian Education took me into his family. After that family moved, another family nearly "adopted"
me. Eventually I moved in with them as part of their
family.

Today I view my adolescence from a different perspective.
It is easy for me to see that I probably would not have
survived but for those wonderful adults making their lives

and love available to me. They tuned into me in such a way
that it literally saved my life.

UNCONDITIONAL ACCEPTANCE

The late psychologist Abraham Maslow said that we have
a hierarchy of needs, which must be met sequentially.
However, I believe there is one need that is almost
instinctual.

Former minister and psychologist Dr. Carl Rogers suggested that people have a desperate need for unconditional acceptance. In fact, he suggested that we are driven
by our need for it. If we do not find it one place, we look
for it in another. I believe that this need is the basis for a
large portion of promiscuity, divorce, and the growth of
religious cults. It probably also influences the high incidence of drug use among both adolescents and adults
today.

If parents can provide an atmosphere for unconditional
acceptance, the search for it will probably end at home. If
parents are unable to provide that atmosphere, then the
search will go elsewhere. Unfortunately, the commodity of
unconditional acceptance is difficult if not impossible to
find. Therefore, the search never ends for some.

Much has been written about the phenomenon of multiple personality. This phenomenon occurs when one person develops more than one identifiable "intact" identity.
These various identities usually have different names, values, and sometimes even are composed of different genders.

Although I have first-hand knowledge of only one professional case of multiple personality, I have read of many.
I describe this phenomenon as related to unconditional
acceptance. If I am not accepted as Jim, then I will become
Tom. If Tom is not sufficient, I will become Henry.

Although that view can be debated, the need for unconditional acceptance cannot. In essence, this is the attitude
that tells the adolescent, "I love you regardless of what you
say or do. I will never quit loving you. You are totally
acceptable to me, unequivocally, just as you are."

My wife and I took new marriage vows several years ago.
This time our vows were less rosy and sweet. We admitted

that, trying our best, we would no doubt fail at times; we might be downright hard to live with at other times. In other words we promised to be human and normal, confessing our limitations and frailties.

However, we also vowed that, no matter what, we would not give up on each other. We clearly stated that separation or divorce simply was not an option for us. What a relief! We gave each other permission to be human and took ourselves off the hooks of impossible expectation. It was a tremendously positive experience.

Our adolescents need a parallel commitment. We must tune in and grant them permission to be adolescents. That implies allowing them to err. They need to grasp onto a love that will support them unconditionally, regardless of error. Obviously, that does not mean that we have to approve and applaud all of their behavior. However, our basic love and acceptance of the teenager must never be up for debate. Once they experience that kind of acceptance, they will feel really tuned into.

TUNING IN TO HOPEFULNESS

A sense of hopefulness is necessary for continued emotional growth of our adolescents. This hopefulness is just another by-product resulting from unconditional acceptance. Research indicates that as long as a teenager has hope for the future he probably will not behave in a self-destructive manner. It is only with a perceived loss of hope that suicide becomes a serious option.

TUNING IN BY LISTENING

One of the most powerful ways to tune into an adolescent is through listening. Most teenagers I see in counseling seriously believe they aren't really heard. Sometimes that is obviously true.

There is a chasmic difference between acknowledgement and true listening. That can be easily experimented with by thinking of some superficial conversation you may recently have overheard. In today's hurried society, there is basically no time for listening. It takes hard work and a great deal of time. People merely acknowledge each other as they hurry to keep up with the pace.

To tune in by listening is a different experience than most of us are used to. It involves two parts. The first part is growing close enough to the adolescent for him to trust you. That involves spending time just being around the teenager. Sometimes that will include no interaction at all. At other times it may include interactions of a less serious nature. I spend hours walking with adolescents or shooting basketballs with them. Barriers somehow melt when you get beaten in a game of one-on-one.

It takes that kind of informal time to approach the point where the teenager will trust the adult with more confidential intimate information. When that time arrives, all energy needs to be focused on listening.

Tuning in while listening means all possible energy is focused on the teenager. If there is any distraction, it must be removed. The attitude brought to the sessions is one of unconditional acceptance. While the teenager is talking, it is best that no interruptions occur. If I am listening, I fight every impulse to question or comment on what he is saying.

Often, no response is necessary. At other times, a mere emphatic reply will be enough. "Wow. Sounds like you're under a lot of pressure," is one example. On occasion it may be important to clarify your understanding of what the teenager has said. This needs to be approached on a very friendly and low-key basis. "What I think you said was ... Did I hear you correctly?" That is one way of seeking clarification from the speaker.

At other times some action may be required in response to what the adolescent has said. In any case, listening is the key. The secret is in being accepting, uncritical, and nonjudgmental. Becoming absorbed in what the adolescent is saying is the critical part of tuning in to them.

TUNING IN BY GIVING STROKES

This is a rather simple concept. Yet many of us seem to have difficulty with it. Strokes are both verbal and nonverbal messages. Their purpose is to express or extend value to the adolescent. "You look nice today" is a stroke. "I love you" is a stroke. "You did a good job on your room" is another stroke.

We all need strokes, and we prefer the positive kind. Adolescents however have a special need for the reassurance that occurs with this sort of reinforcement. A seventeen-year-old female was brought into counseling by her parents.

"I don't think my dad loves me." She sat almost stubbornly.

"OK," I repeated. "You don't think that he loves you. I wonder what makes you think that."

"I just don't think he does. That's all." She was going through emotional trauma because she didn't feel loved. Later during the session she stated that her father provided for her, acted like he loved her, and that really deep down she thought maybe he did. The problem was that he never said it.

And she did mean *never*. Neither that teenager nor her mother could remember her father's ever verbalizing his love to her. She needed to hear it. Since that time I have heard many teens say the same thing. They want to hear reassurance from their parents. These strokes give them strength. Although teens sometimes may superficially act as though they don't like verbalizations of love, they do.

One concept I heard discussed many years ago was "you get what you stroke." Basically, if you stroke negative behavior, you will get more of it. If you stroke positive behavior, you will get more of that. Parents need to be careful what they stroke or pay attention to. A friend of mine stated that he had interviewed several hundred prison inmates when writing his doctoral dissertation. Over 97 percent of them could recall their parents telling them they would end up in jail some day. They did.

A woman in therapy recalled hearing her mother assert how unlovable she was. As an adult her mother's comment had come true. This woman had been married five times. "I guess mother was correct," she said with a sigh.

An extremely intelligent thirty-year-old man continued changing jobs incessantly. He never stayed long enough to really advance. His resume made him look like a drifter. "Mother always told me I would never amount to anything," he explained.

Parental messages, or strokes, need to consist of positive encouragement for adolescent personality development to prosper.

TUNING IN BY RECOGNIZING INDIVIDUAL DIFFERENCES

One of the biggest mistakes parents can make is to expect siblings to be alike. It is an unfair expectation. Actually, individual differences should be encouraged in siblings, especially if they are close together in age. As parents, we need to assure that each of our children has a sense of unique identity.

Surprisingly, that process can be more difficult if the adolescent is unusually attractive or intelligent. People who are gifted in either of those areas never experience the need to struggle. Depth of personality and identity is built when the adolescent is faced with challenge and forced to work. Many attractive adolescent females lead almost charmed lives. That is not to their advantage. While working in a counseling center in Burbank, California, I received a visit from a lady who had been in various television programs and movies. I recognized her immediately but tried not to disclose it.

"I don't have a personality," she lamented. "I just don't have a personality. I have always been given everything I wanted because of my looks. In high school I even got my grades because I was pretty. I have always gotten special treatment just by smiling. I have never had to fight for anything, and I don't even know how."

She was correct. She had few resources at all, other than her appearance. Recently, because of her age and an accident, her appearance had changed. That had been accompanied by the awareness of her weaknesses. Over a period of time she was able to develop the identity and depth she sought.

Parents need to encourage their adolescents to develop not only a unique identity but personal depth. That can come only with struggle. By being forced to work toward a goal that may almost be out of reach, the adolescent learns persistence and determination. Tuning into our adolescents helps provide them with depth.

TUNING IN TO SPIRITUAL INVOLVEMENT

The adolescent's level of spiritual involvement is another key area to tune into. There are a variety of reasons for this, which involve sociological and philosophical factors.

Through the progressive stages of development, the adolescent's spiritual needs will change and probably evolve. They need to be given the freedom to inquire, along with a supportive background to provide strength while searching and exploring. A Christian background and personal belief system can be an important component of emotional health for the teenager.

An involvement in an active church youth program introduces the opportunity for peer relationships to the teenager. Relationships are also more likely to develop with other significant caring adults. In essence, a church can become an extended kinship network for the teenager.

As the adolescent grows spiritually mature, his personality can develop further strength and depth. An added benefit is offered through a sense of hopefulness. An active youth group will provide the adolescent with meaningful activities in which he can become involved. That creates alternatives for stress and tension control and reduces the likelihood of emotional complications. It is important to recall that depression, drug use, and hopelessness are all predictive elements of suicide proneness.

Tuning into our teens' level of spiritual involvement does not mean "cramming religion" down their throats. It is not necessary to do that. As adults we can take the initiative to find the right youth program for the teenager. Once we find it, there will be no need to force the child's attendance. Through attendance and involvement out of personal interest comes another support system and greater opportunity for God's input to be allowed into the teenager's life.

FOR FURTHER THOUGHT

1. Think of a person who has tuned into you. What does he do that makes you feel attended to? List the characteristics of his behavior that give you that impression. What does he say? Can you emulate his behavior?

2. Describe an incident when you tuned into another person. What did you do? How did you feel about it?

3. If an adolescent was to rate you on tuning into him, what would your score be on a scale of 1–10?

4. Think of the music you have heard teenagers listen to. Did you understand what was being said? What does the music mean? If you don't understand, ask a teenager to explain the lyrics to you.

5. Have you ever felt unconditionally accepted? Is there a time that you ever loved someone else unconditionally? How does that feel? Describe the feeling verbally or in writing. If you are close to a teenager, ask that person whether or not he feels accepted unconditionally.

And the King will answer and say to them, Truly I say to you, to the extent that you did it to one of these brothers of Mine, even the least of them, you did it to Me.

—Matthew 25:40

Man's inhumanity to man makes countless thousands mourn!

—Robert Burns

12

SUICIDE MYTHOLOGY

THE DIFFICULTY WITH DATA

The factual data surrounding suicide is clouded in mystery. Part of the mystery is a result of inconsistent reporting methods and recordkeeping. It is difficult to ascertain, as an example, just what the actual suicide rate is. Most statistics are compiled from coroners or other government officials. By talking to police officers, we might get a more accurate picture of what is reality. In one urban area, official statistics indicated that there were no suicides in 1984. However, when police officials from that same community looked into their files they discovered thirteen cases that they considered suicides.

The problem is made more complex because different states and municipalities use different procedures for determining and categorizing suicides. Even within the same jurisdiction, officials often disagree over whether death is accidental, suicide, or homicide. For example, how is a corpse found floating in a river to be categorized?

Another factor that clouds official statistics is community attitudes. Few family members want to admit that their adolescent has committed suicide. As a result, a true suicide may be identified as accidental death. Society, unfortunately, still attaches a stigma not only to those who attempt suicide but also to surviving family members. We will never know the real proportion suicide has reached. We can only generalize. It is safe to say it is a national crisis.

The data listed in this chapter is gathered from various sources. Published sources sometimes contradict each other and themselves. There certainly is no intent to deceive. However, some material is out-of-date and therefore inaccurate by the time it is published.

Nothing can be done to reverse the dilemma. But we can look at the trends, and that is the purpose of this chapter. By focusing on the factual data, we can help eradicate the myths of suicide.

THE STIGMA OF SUICIDE

There is evidence that suicide has occurred throughout recorded history. Although some cultures have recognized and accepted altruistic suicide at various times, it has generally been discouraged, condemned, and even in some instances considered illegal.

In ancient Roman law suicide was considered a crime. American, English, and most European legal systems have their common origins in Roman law. The stigma often attached to suicide during those ancient civilizations persists today. In fact, suicide is still a crime in parts of our country. Life insurance companies share a similar value and, in some cases, refuse to compensate families of suicide victims.

As a result of the society norm against suicide, the family of a victim often feels blamed for the act. In many ways the family feels it has violated some unspoken rule. The stigma the family experiences is a result of various societal myths surrounding suicide. It is to be hoped that this chapter will clarify some of those legends.

ALCOHOL AND DRUGS

There appears to be a close connection between suicide attempts and drug usage. In 1984 more than 80 percent of all reported teenage suicides had alcohol in their systems. Nearly 90 percent of all teenagers will experiment with alcohol or drugs before age fourteen.

One in five successful suicides is committed by a person who suffers from chronic alcoholism. Accidental deaths occur twice as often among alcoholics and drug addicts. It is estimated that a majority of those deaths may be suicide. Drug addicts are 350 percent more likely to commit suicide than are nonaddicted individuals of the same age.

PHYSICAL ABUSE

More than 70 percent of all adolescent suicide attempters have experienced either physical abuse or serious neglect within three months of the suicide attempt.

NATIONAL TOTALS

Suicide is the second-leading cause of death among teenagers. It is estimated that approximately 6,000 adolescents will take their lives annually. If all age groups are included, that number climbs to 30,000 successful suicides per year. During the past twenty-five years the teenage rate has tripled. One report indicates that nearly 12 percent of all school children will experience serious suicidal ideation at least once. Each day more than thirteen people between the ages of fifteen and twenty-four will take their lives.

Since 1970 the suicide rate for adolescents has risen 44 percent while increasing less than 3 percent in the nation as a whole. In that same time period suicide has increased from the fifth-leading cause of death among teenagers to the second-leading cause. Dr. Seymour Perlin, chairman of the board of the new Youth Suicide National Center in Washington, D.C., states that 2,000,000 adolescents between the ages of fifteen and nineteen will attempt suicide in the coming year.

FAMILY PROBLEM

Suicide appears to be a family problem. It was stated earlier that most teenagers who take their lives come from troubled homes. The importance of parent-child relationships has already been discussed. Adolescents who have attempted suicide often express profound feelings of abandonment and despair concerning their families. The largest portion of those who attempt suicide come from either single parent families or from homes with a parent or parents who are "psychologically absent."

Divorced or widowed adults are more likely to commit suicide than married adults. Happily married adults are less likely than members of problem marriages.

DISCUSSING SUICIDE

More than 70 percent of those who attempt suicide give verbal or nonverbal clues. Most often, if someone is listening, the potential attempter will discuss it. Similarly, discussing suicide prevention will not plant the idea. Indeed it will reduce the possibility of the adolescent's taking his life. Teenagers already have the idea. Demystifying suicide by discussing it can remove some of its power.

INDIVIDUAL DIFFERENCES

One study found some differences between adolescents who attempted or threatened suicide and those who did not. Suicidal attempters shared: (1) a greater preoccupation with death; (2) more depression and recent aggression; (3) more depression in parents; and (4) more suicidal impulses in the mother.

Another study found suicidal children also displayed more aggression toward themselves (or more self-punishing behavior). They also had a history of physical altercations with others. In an additional study, suicide attempters were less likely to cry or exhibit pain responses, even after real accidents that normally would have resulted in outbursts of painful crying.

A recent research project at the University of California at Berkley has discovered that among the general population (including adults) the strongest factor predicting suicide is the severity of previous attempts. For example, someone who had shot himself was more likely to make a second attempt than someone who had taken an overdose of aspirin. Other critical factors in that study included: sexual orientation (bisexuals and homosexuals are more likely to commit suicide than heterosexuals); recent stressful events; financial trouble or loss; feelings of being persecuted; and sharp weight gain or weight loss.

A 1974 report supported the thesis that adolescent suicide attempters fail to feel close to adults. Other factors in this report included a longstanding history of problems from early childhood; an escalation of problems beyond those typically experienced by adolescents; an inability to cope with overwhelming experiences; a dissolving of meaningful social relationships in the time immediately preceding the attempt; and a rationalization that enables the adolescent to justify his suicide attempt.

Another study looked at suicide motivation in adolescents. That inquiry found that school and family constitute the two major sources of tension that lead to self-destruction. A closer look at school-related suicides reveals, however, that the pressure is often the result of unrealistic academic expectations placed on the child's performance by overly demanding parents. The same study also revealed that boys in the above cases were often involved with successful and demanding fathers who stressed school success and hypermasculinity.

A final report indicated growing up in a hostile or emotionally impoverished environment where neglect, rejection, and marital conflict abound may also contribute to suicide-proneness. That could certainly foster feelings of helplessness and lead to despair.

DEPRESSION

Depression appears to be a factor in successful suicides. In fact, it is possibly one of the strongest factors. Also, as mentioned earlier, a history of depression in the family of the adolescent may be a primary predictor.

CLUSTERS

Clustering or "copycat suicide" is indeed a trend. The most obvious clusters seem to occur in middle to upper class and relatively new suburbs. The copycat phenomenon apparently results from an implicit but recognized permission from one suicide to commit another. "Permission" may be needed for some attempters to go against the taboo of suicide.

Clear Lake City, Texas, a suburb of Houston, experienced six suicides in three months. Chattanooga, Tennessee, experienced nine in four months. The affluent West Chester, Rockland, and Putnam counties north of New York City were the setting for twelve deaths. A major cluster occurred in Plano, Texas, a suburb of Dallas. Within fifteen months Plano had a total of eight adolescent suicides.

No one really can explain the dynamics operating in those situations. However, most family counselors and sociologists generalize what they believe is a unique community stress. In most of the communities just mentioned, there is a high transient population. People are not given an opportunity to plant roots. Plano, as an example, has grown from a small community of 30,000 to a sprawling suburb of 100,000 in a brief ten-year span.

The high level of divorce in those areas is also mentioned as a factor. Chattanooga, as an example, had approximately 2,300 marriages in 1983, yet more than 2,400 divorces in the same year. That would naturally lead to a large number of single-parent families.

A third element may be the large number of dual-career families, which may lead to children's not receiving the quantity of attention they need. This is usually a response to economic factors such as increased inflation. In areas with a declining economy, unemployment or underemployment could be a cause. The consequent stress experienced by a parent is easily sensed by the adolescent.

Serious pressure to perform, sometimes placed on adolescents by middle- and upper-middle-class families, was also suggested as a consideration. Often these parents place expectations on the adolescent completely out of proportion to reality. When the child does not live up to the parents' unrealistic standards, he feels defeated and abandoned.

A final reason could possibly be the absence in those communities of the extended family. Adolescents seem to find tremendous strength in the presence of extended kinship networks. With a high transient population and the absence of this network, the adolescent is stripped of an extremely valuable resource.

THE SEASONS OF SUICIDE

Most suicides occur in April or May. December has the lowest rate except around Christmas. There are a large number of suicides during the Thanksgiving, Christmas, and New Year holiday periods. Suicides occur most frequently on Friday and Monday. Sunday runs a strong third. Three times more women attempt suicide than men. On the other hand, three times more men actually succeed. Men use more violent means to commit suicide including the use of guns and explosives and by hanging. People with serious depressive reactions are 500 times more likely to commit suicide than the general population.

More professionals commit suicide than others. Farm workers have the lowest incidence among occupational groups. Dentists and physicians take their lives at the rate of 6 1/2 to 1 over the general population. Lawyers commit suicide at a ratio of 5 to 1 over the general population.

MULTIPLE ATTEMPTS

A common mistake is to consider the individual who attempts suicide but fails as not really serious, or that the person is just doing it to get attention. Actually, that is not the case. Studies show that approximately 15 percent of those who attempt and fail at suicide initially will make a second successful attempt within two years. According to one report, approximately 80 percent of all successful suicides had been preceded by a previous attempt or overt threat.

GROUP DIFFERENCES

Suicide is much higher in highly urbanized and industrialized societies. The rate is higher in times of a poor economy. It is also higher in densely populated cities than in rural areas. The rate is much higher among whites than blacks and higher yet among Orientals.

Protestants have higher suicide rates than Catholics. Catholics have higher rates than Jewish people. Men are more prone to suicide than women. College students are more likely to commit suicide than nonstudents of the same age

American Indians have a suicide rate five times higher than the national average. Most suicide attempts by American Indians occur among teenagers, particularly males. The causes may include the unique struggle facing those young men when presented with the incredibly dramatic conflict between tribal values and those of mainstream America. To the young American Indian it may appear there are limited opportunities in either society. This could be another manifestation of hopelessness.

Minority groups, in general, have additional stress facing them. The largest portion of this stress is attributed to a higher incidence of poverty and a sometimes more frequent absence of the father figure.

THE TYPICAL ATTEMPTER AND VICTIM

In a 1970 study, the "typical" suicide attempter was found to be a Caucasian female housewife in her early thirties, who attempted to kill herself by swallowing barbituates and claimed marital difficulty or depression as the reason.

That was contrasted with the typical person who would succeed at suicide. This person would be a Caucasian Protestant male, in his forties or older, who lived in an urban environment. He was probably divorced or separated from his family and committed suicide by shooting, hanging, or by carbon monoxide poisoning. The reasons for the death were ill health, depression, marital difficulty, or hopelessness.

However, according to a recent news report, to be more accurate today the gender and age of the typical suicide attempter would need to be changed to a female adolescent. The successful suicide victim would be a male adolescent.

GENERAL SIMILARITIES

I have dealt with a large number of people who had attempted suicide as adolescents and adults. There are several factors they hold in common.

Most of them describe a history of depression, often dating from early childhood. There is usually an origin of the depression in either unexpressed or inappropriately expressed anger. Relationships with extended family are poor. This typically includes parents. The father figure is generally absent or emotionally distant.

A majority among this group confess unfulfilled dreams or not living up to expectations. They consider themselves underachievers, misplaced, or underutilized. If employed, they consider themselves underemployed and are dissatified with their jobs.

There is a common history of unsatisfying interpersonal relationships. They are usually from single-parent homes. If they are adults, there is likely to be a divorce in the recent past. It is also common for them to have recent conflict with authority figures, including law enforcement personnel. All of those factors lead to a generalized loneliness.

Most suicide attempts do have precipitating factors. However, the precipitating factor alone is not the cause of the self-destructive act. It is only one of accumulating reasons in the process leading to suicide attempts. The precipitating factor can be interpersonal conflict, employment difficulty, or any of a wide variety of problems. Yet, behind the precipitating event is a long history of emotional trauma and unresolved turmoil. In other words, a person's decision toward suicide may be tipped by an otherwise unexceptional event. But the event itself is only the tip of the iceberg.

The common factors, then, are believed to include deep sense of hopelessness, helplessness, and loneliness. These people see little alternative to death. Life seems empty, meaningless, and wasteful. The attempt is usually a desperate act by someone seeking relief from pain. Unfortunately, the consequences of an attempt usually make things worse.

BIBLICAL SUICIDES

The Bible records very few examples of suicide, and we have no accurate records as to the suicide rate during the biblical period of our history. Seven actual suicides are recorded, and each will be briefly discussed and documented.

JUDAS

The best-known example is that of Judas. Following his betrayal of Jesus in the Garden of Gethsemane he came to the realization of what he had done. Feeling remorseful and condemned he returned his "blood money" to the chief priests, and Matthew 27:5 says he went and hanged himself. Acts 1:18 specifies even further the details surrounding his death.

ZIMRI

Zimri, who reigned as king of Israel for only seven days, set fire to the citadel of the king's house and burned both the house and himself to death. That act was upon realizing that his rule was being overthrown by the commander of the army of Israel (1 Kings 16:18).

AHITHOPHEL

Ahithophel was a counselor of David, king of Israel. He had conspired with David's son, Absalom, to overthrow David's throne. When his plans were not followed, the Bible says he "saddled his donkey and arose . . . went . . . home, set his house in order, and strangled himself" (2 Samuel 17:23).

ABIMELECH

Abimelech, son of Gideon, was made king after killing his sixty-nine half-brothers, who were possible heirs to the throne. During an attempted conquest of the tower of the city of Thebez, a woman threw a large stone, which hit Abimelech's head and crushed his skull. Abimelech quickly called his armorbearer and instructed him to thrust his sword through Abimelech, lest someone say that a woman had killed him (Judges 9:53, 54).

SAUL

Another king of Israel, Saul, fell on his own sword and killed himself after losing a battle against the Philistines. Saul had requested his armorbearer to slay him, but he refused. However, once the armorbearer saw that his king was dead, he also fell on his own sword and killed himself. Thus, one suicide influenced another, as we see occurring today in clusters of suicide (1 Samuel 31:4–5; 1 Chronicles 10:4–5).

SAMSON

The final biblical example is that of Samson. His case differs somewhat from the others in that he not only killed himself but simultaneously caused the death of 3,000 Philistines. Perhaps the strongest man who ever lived, his power was weakened when he stopped allowing God to direct his life. Revealing his source of strength resulted in his loss of power and his subsequent capture. The Philistines humiliated him and used him for sport at their gatherings. Eventually, he pulled down (under his own regained power) the supporting pillars of the building where 3,000 were gathered. Thus he sacrificed himself along with his captors (Judges 16:25–30).

DISCUSSION

Following a suicide, family members struggle to cope with overwhelming pain. Their pain goes beyond that of losing a loved one to ordinary death. It includes coping with shame and humiliation surrounding a suicide. In addition, families agonize over the question of whether the suicide victim will now suffer eternally.

The Bible says that salvation is a gift of God, not something one earns or deserves (Ephesians 2:8). Therefore, we can do nothing to say we deserve it, as discovered in Mark 10:17–21. Salvation is not earned by works; it is accepted as a gift.

A second factor is mentioned in John 10:27–29:

> My sheep hear my voice and I know them, and they follow me; and I give eternal life to them, and they shall never perish; and no one shall snatch them out of my hand. My Father, who has given them to me, is greater than all; and no one is able to snatch them out of the Father's hand.

Christ teaches in this passage that He gives eternal life. And once He gives that assurance of salvation, no man can take it away, by any measure.

Biblical scholars believe that if a person's life has demonstrated faith through obedience, it will result in evidence of the fruits of the Spirit (Galatians 5:22–23): "But the fruit of the Spirit is love, joy, peace, patience, kindness, goodness, faithfulness, gentleness, self-control."

Evidence of the fruit of the Spirit is indication that a person is living in the grace of God.

Sometimes human emotions can become overwhelming and obscure a previous view of reality. At such a point one's judgment can obviously be affected. When someone inflicts his own death, there is not an opportunity to make retribution. However, in 1 Samuel 16:7 God tells Samuel that He judges in a different manner than humans: "God sees not as man sees, for man looks at the outward appearance, but the Lord looks at the heart."

That implies that an omniscient God would have awareness beyond suicide. As humans, we do not have that same evidence to weigh. Neither can we fully examine all the factors God weighs. But going back to our first reference, John 10:27–29, God says that once He has given eternal life as a gift, it cannot be taken away.

FOR FURTHER THOUGHT

1. What do you believe are God's expectations of us in responding to suicide attempters and their families? Where does judgment of a suicide attempt play a part? Reflect on your own attitude toward attempted suicide. Are you satisfied with it?

2. If someone you knew attempted suicide, how would you respond to that person? If that person were a close friend or relative? Or your own teenager? Consider what you would say or do.

3. How does your own community involve itself with families and victims of either suicide or attempts? Are you satisfied with the level and kind of involvement? Decide how you can contribute to the church's involvement.

4. Try to imagine the feelings of attempted suicide victims and their families. If you were in their shoes, what would you need from others?

5. After reading this chapter, what is your level of concern with adolescent suicide and potential suicide? What will you do about it? Reflect on any changes in your ideas or thoughts concerning the problem of suicide as a result of what you have read.

For I was hungry, and you gave Me something to eat; I was thirsty, and you gave Me drink. I was a stranger, and you invited me in; naked, and you clothed Me; I was sick, and you visited Me; I was in prison, and you came to Me.

—Matthew 25:35-36

You must look into people as well as at them.

—Philip Dormer Stanhope

13

CHATTANOOGA: A MODEL FOR COMMUNITY INTERVENTION

The purpose of this chapter is to provide an outline for other communities. The specific factors that were operational in Chattanooga would not necessarily operate the same elsewhere. However, the outline of how our intervention was designed and promoted may be useful to others.

I mentioned in a previous chapter that my father told me as I stared at a diving tower to "just do it . . . go ahead and make the dive and not worry about the form." In many ways that was my philosophy as I approached the intervention in Chattanooga. I had never taken part in a community effort of that sort and had little idea of what needed to occur. However a major problem had surfaced in our community, and somebody had to *just do it.*

The Problem

As mentioned in chapter 1, I was uniquely aware of the suicide problem in Chattanooga. My awareness evolved over a period of time. Because of the nature of my profession, a number of people often call and ask me if I have

heard about recent suicide attempts or some other tragedy. That happens so frequently that my wife can detect
when I have received such calls without my mentioning it.

During the period of September 1984 to January 1985 I
had received an unusual number of such calls. I have a
close friend who is a police official. He and I frequently
had discussed the apparent increase in suicide during that
time. However, for whatever reason, it alarmed neither of
us to the point of wanting to make any public response.
Yet we both found it unusual.

On several occasions my colleague Dr. Ross Campbell
and I discussed what seemed to be a large number of
adolescent appointments in our office during that same
period. He is usually booked ahead several weeks anyway,
but during this period we received an unusually large number of calls.

Other professional staff members at our counseling center and colleagues at other counseling centers were also
reporting a large number of appointments. One public
agency had established a six-week waiting list for appointments.

Somehow, we all shrugged it off.

THE DEVELOPMENT OF THE ISSUE

I am sure it occurred within a longer period of time, but
looking back it seems that within a matter of days tragedies
began to multiply. First, a father in his mid-thirties shot
himself as he sat in his car. He left his wife and infant
children. Two men jumped off local bridges into the Tennessee River on the same day. One died, the other survived. Then the two teenagers at the local high school
committed suicide. Another person jumped from the bridge.

By that time our secretaries had been flooded with calls.
Most of our regular appointments had been put off until
we could handle the emergencies. On one particular afternoon Dr. Campbell admitted four adolescents to area hos-
pitals for observation.

We all were touched by the tragedies. During one discussion we both agreed something had to be done. We
knew it had to be a very large intervention to end the

epidemic of suicides. It was essential that we get the attention of the entire community.

Chattanooga is a very caring, very friendly city. Generally, the people can be expected to be responsive and loving. I have described the series of events as if they were publicly noticed. They were not. That was part of the problem. The community at large was only aware of the two bridge jumps. That was because those events were covered by the media. Had I not been in the particular profession I am, I also would have been unaware of the large increase in suicides.

My pastor and I met at breakfast one morning and discussed the nature of the community problem. We agreed something needed to be done. He offered the use of the church as a base open to the public. That seemed a good idea at the time, but we were not sure what event we should hold there. We also questioned whether or not having it at the church would exclude a certain element of the population. He recommended I talk to various people from the media. Within days I had met with representatives from local TV, radio, and newspapers.

An idea was beginning to take shape. We started considering the possibility of a panel discussion. A variety of people would be included on the panel. A local TV station agreed to sponsor and promote it. There were only dim hopes that the community would become involved. "It's too depressing a topic," someone suggested. Yet when I mentioned the idea to Dr. Campbell, he responded favorably. He also proposed we contact our Congresswoman, Mrs. Marilyn Lloyd.

She agreed to address the meeting that we were going to hold. That fact got the local media more interested in the problem. Newspaper articles began to appear. In late February a large article was printed concerning the responsibility of churches to respond to the local suicide epidemic. Three weeks later a follow-up article appeared in the same newspaper. A few days afterward, the competing area newspaper joined in.

THE PANEL

Meanwhile, a highly rated newscaster in the area had agreed to host and moderate the panel. The members were chosen, and the panel began to take shape. We chose the particular panel members we did for several reasons. Each of them had a specific area of expertise that was vital. However, there are a large number of experts in any community. In addition to their expertise, I recognized that we needed people with visibility. We needed people that the public would be willing not only to listen to, but to come out and see.

For all those reasons the panel consisted of, first of all, Dr. Campbell. Dr. Campbell is a noted author, lecturer, and psychiatrist. He is an expert in child and adolescent psychiatry and an excellent psychotherapist. A local pastor was the second person who agreed to be on the panel. In addition to being the pastor of one of Chattanooga's largest churches, he was additionally a family counselor and acutely aware of adolescent problems. Not only was he visible in the community, he was a source of spiritual counsel and was able to offer biblical viewpoints. It is important that the voice of the Christian community be heard on such an issue. The public information officer of the Chattanooga Police Department was the next person to agree to join the panel. He was very active in media affairs. He was also an expert in statistics and very familiar with the local problem. The next panelist was the drug information officer for the sheriff's department, an ordained minister. He was very active in the community and an expert in alcohol and drug abuse. He was well aware of the suicide problem, especially among alcoholics and drug addicts. I included myself on the panel because of my professional background and public visibility through radio, television, and public speaking.

By this time a commitment had been made. The date was set. A location was chosen. The membership of the panel had agreed to serve. The problem was publicity. All the media experts were still pessimistic and had informed me it was a long shot. The odds were certainly against its being well attended.

I was somewhat naive and ill-informed about media and public meetings of this sort. I realized promotion was necessary. However, I was totally unaware of the magnitude of what I had begun.

RESEARCH

During our preparation for the meeting my wife was doing technical research. She spent hours in the library and even more hours on the phone. Dr. Campbell conducted his own research and prepared a brochure for distribution to people who attended the seminar. Congresswoman Lloyd sent a general mailing to area members of her congressional district. Letters were sent to clergymen in the community making them aware of the panel. The local office of the YMCA sent letters to all their members in the surrounding area. Area high schools distributed announcements to students and teachers and promoted attendance. The local Mental Health Association agreed to help sponsor the symposium and also distributed announcements throughout the area.

As the date of the forum neared, the pace of preparation rose to a frantic level. There were calls from newspapers throughout the state. Television stations from surrounding cities requested interviews. The Associated Press distributed stories of the forum throughout the country. One week before the panel, television and radio stations began airing promotions that were played throughout the broadcast day. The day before the symposium I appeared live on the 6:00 P.M. news. The following morning I appeared at 6:00 A.M. on a morning talk show and at 8:30 A.M. on a popular radio program. At 7:30 P.M. the symposium was scheduled to begin.

I held my breath.

LEARN BY DOING

Those of us primarily involved in planning the symposium made several mistakes but learned a great deal from the experience. It would be helpful for anyone planning such an event to consider the following points:

1. Public relations for an effort of this sort is probably at least as important as what transpires during the meeting. I had no idea of the task we faced attempting to get the public to attend the symposium. A public relations expert needs to work on a project of this nature exclusively for a period of six to ten weeks. The meeting is futile if nobody attends.
2. Media involvement is absolutely essential. Without it the entire project would have failed. Also realize that media is a competitive business. I made a decision to work with one particular television station primarily because I had cooperated with it on other projects. It happened to be the top-rated television station in this area. Just as television stations compete against each other, they also compete against radio and print journalism. That is where experts in public relations can be of benefit. If you are not sure where to turn, you might end up where you don't want to be!
3. Your approach to publicity must be multifaceted. We utilized newspapers, television, radio, word of mouth, direct mail, schools, churches, and our congressional representative to spread the word.
4. Someone has to push. There needs to be at least one person who keeps things rolling. Because of ongoing responsibilities by most persons involved, there must be one person to coordinate media activity and to make certain the deadlines are met.
5. Expect to be inconvenienced by other people's deadlines. There were literally hundred of deadlines before our meeting. Taping, recording, printing, scripts, teleprompters, and so on. I requested the media to become involved. It was my responsibility to work around their schedules.
6. It is important to share information. The research my wife gathered and typed was given to all panel members to help them in their own preparation. Additionally, I helped to write the promotions for radio and television. I also provided a list of questions and an outline to the moderator of the panel.
7. Good intentions are not enough. Neither is skill or knowledge. It really does take more. I could have

assembled the world's leading experts and had ten people attend the symposium. Marketing is what will bring in the participants.

8. Be sure to coordinate logistical efforts. We ended up in a filled auditorium on a hot spring night with no air conditioning. With time it became increasingly uncomfortable for some.

9. Choose a public meeting place rather than a church. Some people simply will not attend a meeting held in a church. Also, you could effectively eliminate certain denominational segments by your choice of churches.

10. Choose an auditorium that is neither too large nor too small. It may be better to choose one too small. A crowd can appear large or small depending on the meeting place. It is much better for the panel to have a large crowd in a small room than a small crowd in a large room.

11. Include experts from a variety of backgrounds on the panel. We could have used some of the leading psychiatrists, psychologists, and counselors in the community to take part in the panel. However, by getting panelists from a variety of fields, we increased the level of general interest from the community.

12. Include clergy in your planning. They not only have a great deal of skill and knowledge, they also work on a daily basis with people who are troubled and in pain. The clergy is an extremely valuable resource and can offer spiritual counsel.

13. Get local government officials to assist you. Our entire effort would have failed had not Congresswoman Lloyd endorsed it. When she expressed an interest, the media immediately perked up with interest. Not only was her mailing of assistance but also her general level of input throughout the community.

14. Gain the support of your local Mental Health Association. They can be of tremendous assistance in any project of this nature.

THE SYMPOSIUM

The symposium took place on schedule. The auditorium was packed. Folding chairs had to be distributed. The entire first row was filled with press representatives. Some people even had to stand up in the back of the auditorium.

The response during the symposium and afterwards was extremely positive. We distributed cards so that people could write down any questions they had. Over 300 such cards were returned, many with more than one question. More than 100 of those who filled out cards asked for a similar meeting in the future.

Since the symposium, the suicides in Chattanooga have decreased. We are not sure why. Perhaps the symposium did have some impact. It is likely though that media involvement made the greatest impact. Whereas in the symposium we reached those who attended, the influence of TV, radio, and newspaper reached far beyond that.

We live in a community. Community awareness and involvement cannot be minimized. When the community became involved, life improved for everybody. It happened here. It can happen nationwide.

The famous commercial and advertising slogan has the right idea.

"Reach out," we are told. "Reach out and touch someone. Reach out, and just say hi."

It will work. One person who cares can save a life.

There is hope.

SUMMARY

The purpose of this chapter was to provide guidance for other communities who are interested in making a similar intervention. The history of development of the problem was discussed to give understanding of why an intervention was indicated.

The symposium in our community was successful. A similar symposium could be equally as needed and effective in your community. Informed, concerned citizens can make a significant difference in saving even one life.

FOR FURTHER THOUGHT

1. Do you see a need for a similar symposium in your community? Who are key persons you can contact concerning such a need? As an involved citizen, what can you personally offer?

2. After discussing the need with key persons, is there a person you can recommend as a candidate for coordinator? After enlisting a coordinator, how can you help toward the effort? Whom do you know personally who would also be willing to help?

3. Using steps outlined in this chapter, what needs to be done next? What are your goals and criteria for a symposium to prevent suicides in your community?

4. Think of your own responsibility. Is a symposium an effort you can begin on your own? If not, why?

5. Contact your local Mental Health Association. Inquire as to whether they have educational programs similar to the one described in this chapter. If not, suggest they begin one.

6. Contact your local school system. If it has no program to educate teachers, encourage its leaders to design one.

APPENDIX

Frequently I have the opportunity to be on television and radio talk shows nationwide. I have been interviewed by national news services. Various organizations have invited me to speak or hold seminars. The ostensible subject of those appearances has been teenage suicide and other crises of adolescence.

As a result, I have been asked hundreds of questions both in person and through the mail. Many of the questions are similar. I have chosen to respond to those I receive most frequently. These are questions asked, in one form or another, at each appearance I make. Many of the topics have already been discussed generally in one of the chapters of this book.

Question: In your opinion, what do you think is the most important factor in preventing suicide?

Answer: There are various considerations mentioned in different studies and research projects. The one that seems to persist in its impact, however, is the importance of the parent-child relationship. If it is one of warmth, support, and love, the child has a tremendous resource of strength. It gives the child hope.

The one consistent symptom in most suicides appears to be a sense of hopelessness. Teenagers and adults alike seem to lose hope when faced with depleted social resources. That may also be a component of loneliness. If the parents are absent, that can probably be compensated for by intense relationships with other significant adults. However, in most cases, adults need to take the initiative to form those relationships.

Hope also originates from faith in Jesus Christ, especially in late adolescents. However, most early teenagers are still functioning from a more concrete style of thinking. In comparison, theological thought is very abstract. Unless that thought is balanced by the experience of living the Christlike life, establishing a positive relationship with God is impossible. A correspondingly positive relationship with parents helps the adolescent to understand and bridge that gap. The leap between concrete and abstract thought is one that requires sequential steps and a great deal of transition time. Those are best facilitated through a strong and supportive relationship with caring parents or involved significant adults.

Virtually all contributing factors toward the recent suicide trend can eventually be traced and connected to the child's relationship with his parents and other significant adults. If those relationships are strong, the child can find strength and stability to face practically any crisis. As in my own life, other adults can fill in if parental relationships are taken from a child.

Of all findings from research today, the stable, caring, parental or significant adult-teen relationship appears to be the most powerful factor in preventing suicide attempts.

Question: Is there any evidence of a higher incidence of teenage suicide where the mother has outside employment? What about broken homes?

Answer: To answer the first question, I have found no evidence, either personally or through research, of a higher incidence of suicide in families with a working mother. That mother works outside the home is not really an issue. On the other hand, the quality of the parent-child relationship is definitely a factor. If the working mother can maintain a close supportive relationship with her children, there simply is no evidence to say her children are at higher risk of suicide.

With regard to broken homes, there is definite evidence that children from broken homes have a higher incidence of suicide. The risk is decreased if the child has appropriate caring relationships with other adults. That statistic is certainly not a reflection on the quality of single parenting. It is more a commentary on the needs of teenagers. Their social needs are so complex and demanding that one parent alone is just not equipped to meet all of them. When assisted by an extended social network, however, the burden is reduced.

Question: Can short attention span and boredom be symptoms of depression for adults as well as teenagers? If not, what are the symptoms to look for in adults?

Answer: In many ways the symptoms are similar, especially in young adults. Generally, it is easier to notice depression as people grow older. Adolescents will more readily attempt to mask or disguise despair. Short attention span and boredom are two symptoms to look for in adults. There are also other red-flag symptoms. Most diagnostic criteria suggest that depression in adults may be present if a combination of any three symptoms exist and persist for a minimum of two weeks. The most common symptoms are:

Lack of sleep or chronic sleepiness
Low energy level
Feelings of inadequacy
Decreased effectiveness at school, work, or home
Social withdrawal
Loss of interest in pleasurable activities
Excessive anger
Inability to respond with pleasure to praise or rewards
Less talkative than usual
Pessimistic attitude toward future
Unusual crying or tearfulness
Preoccupation with death or suicide

Loss of interest in sex
Chronic guilt
Feeling slowed down
Brooding about past events

In adults, depression is most commonly noticed by an attitude of sadness and a report of feeling blue. The primary difference between adolescents and adults is that adults more easily manifest the sadness.

Question: I believe that a lot of problems are a result of TV programming. For example, in most instances the actor or actress meets a gigantic problem, and within one hour that person solves it. That seldom happens in real life. Solving a problem usually takes more time. What can we do to change TV programming?

Answer: There is a natural human tendency to search for concrete answers to problems. Unfortunately, the challenges we face today are so complex that there are few easy or concrete solutions. The causes of suicide are so complicated we cannot narrow them to one in particular.

TV programming is obviously influential. The unrealistic portrayal of problem resolution can present teenagers and adults with a tremendous sense of inadequacy. Even some of the families presented on television are so idealized that the rest of us feel parentally impotent in comparison. Realism has been portrayed on television. However, it apparently is not well received. Quite frankly, it appears the American public prefers escapism to realism.

TV programmers do indeed respond to viewer ratings. The ratings are far more important than public responses through the mail or threatened boycotts. That is because advertising cost is directly proportional to the rating of any particular program.

One person, or even a local group, will never change programming. The only way to influence an organization the size of a TV network is through ratings. Refusing to watch a particular show will decrease its effect on you as an individual viewer. If enough people do that (realizing that there needs to be an extremely large number), the show will be dropped. In summary, turning the TV off will help.

Question: What is the cause of all the anger we have heard and read about in young people?

Answer: That is a very complex question. There may not be one particular cause. However, there is room for a few generalizations.

First, it is quite normal in modern society for people to respond with anger. There are some cultures in which people do not experience such an emotion. One well researched example recently described is the Tasaday Indians of the Philippines. Apparently, in their particular tribal language there is not even a word to describe the emotion of anger. Nevertheless, in modern society, anger is a typical response. To put it another way, anger is normal. The problem with anger is more profound with teens because of pressure placed on them by some adults to deny their anger. That tendency to act as if it does not exist creates greater latent anger. When a teenager is made to feel guilty about his anger, fuel is only added to the fire. There are then two negative emotions to cope with instead of one. Guilt not only magnifies the problem. It can evolve and erupt into anger itself.

Some think there is an added factor to consider. The pendulum appears to be swinging toward a more harsh approach to childrearing, especially among some elements of society. Extremely rigid parenting systems are as destructive as the formerly popular permissive systems. Teens can achieve their highest potential and remain less angry in a system of well-balanced, flexible structure.

Another contributing factor to the anger of today's youth is the perpetual and overwhelming pace of change. Internal changes are occurring rapidly in individual development. The complexity of those changes is increased because of their inconsistency. A teen can be physically mature, yet cognitively or emotionally immature. This disparity is extremely disconcerting.

At the same time, external or environmental changes

occur so rapidly it is almost impossible to keep up. Sociologists have come to refer to this phenomenon as the hurried society. Adults experience a great deal of difficulty adapting to the hurried society. Adolescents are even more baffled. One common result of essentially taking one step forward and two back is frustration or anger.

All of those factors combine to influence a generation of adolescents having a tremendous amount of anger. When unexpressed, it most often results in depression. It also leads to disillusionment with authority figures including parents, schools, and formal religion.

Although I have no research on which to base my next comment, my intuition is that this disillusionment is one big influence on the parallel increase of drug use, religious cults, runaways, and suicide. All of those tragic trends parallel a final increase—the number of adolescents dropping out of formal church activity.

With their support systems removed, the anger cycle is perpetuated and accelerated.

Question: Where should you take someone who has made a gesture or attempt at suicide, even if it's a small one?

Answer: First, I need to qualify the terminology. I'm not sure there is such a thing as a small gesture. Obviously, there are degrees of severity. Any movement toward self-destructiveness, however, is very serious in my view.

If there is any possible bodily damage, take the person to an emergency room. It is probably best to get the person checked out medically first. Afterward I would accompany the person to a trained professional who specializes in adolescent treatment, if it is a teenager.

Question: What is our responsibility if an adolescent tells us he is going to commit suicide? Should we go to his parents if we see some problems?

Answer: If someone, especially a child, tells me he is going to commit suicide, I act. I express concern and love for him. I make sure he is not left alone. I remove anything he could use to injure himself. Then I contact an authority

figure. That may be the child's parents. However, I also explain to the child what I am doing and why.
When someone talks about suicide, we had better listen.

Question: How can teenagers help each other? What can we do to keep our friends from committing suicide? I had one girl friend last year who did, and I didn't even know something was wrong. After that, two others tried. I felt awful, and it was like there was nothing I could do.

Answer: You have asked a question that captures the helplessness that we all feel about suicide.
Teenagers can help each other so much. Generally, be a friend to these people. Reach out to them. Encourage them to talk. If you detect a problem, go to a teacher or parent who you know really cares and tell them. Also, familiarize yourself with the signs and symptoms of depression and suicidal behavior.

Question: Is there anything we should not say or do to someone who is threatening suicide? What would be the wrong thing to do?

Answer: There are a few things I would avoid. I would not make fun of somebody who is talking about suicide. I would not challenge that person to go ahead and do it. I also would not ignore him. I think it might be a mistake to try to be a "shrink" and interpret what such a person is saying. There are a lot of things I have seen TV cops do that are absurd.
I take every attempt seriously. I never play games with suicidal behavior.

Question: Does a person have to want help before he can be helped? What can a parent do if a child does not want help?

Answer: I get a lot of phone calls from parents. They say "Billy doesn't want to come to counseling, but I think he needs it. What should I do?"
My response to the parent is, "What would you do if

Billy's appendix ruptured, and he didn't want to go to the hospital? What would you do if his leg was broken, and he didn't want a cast? Would you make him go anyway?"

I think adolescent emotional problems are just as significant. If my children get depressed, I'll take them to the best person I know. If I have to fly them to the opposite coast to see that person, I'll do it.

I would take the child to counseling and let the counselor worry about the child's resistance at being there. That's what counselors are paid to do.

Question: What about those of us who can't afford fees for people like yourself? Are there good places with low fees?

Answer: Yes, there are a number of places with low fees. There is probably a family and children's services agency in your city. These agencies are usually supported by United Fund and provide low-cost counseling. There are mental health centers, churches, and other counseling facilities with very reasonable fees. Some are pro-rated on income; others have a flat fee. Usually, those facilities provide good services.

Question: Do you think there is too much emphasis placed on guilt and meekness in Christian homes? I see so many kids who are too self-effacing and humble. What do you think?

Answer: If a parent is using guilt to discipline a child, I would encourage that parent to reconsider. Unless the parent is certain of what he or she is doing, I would recommend using an alternative method of discipline. Guilt is too dangerous.

You see, I view what is happening from a different perspective than most people. Day in and day out, sometimes twelve or fourteen hours a day, I get to see everybody's mistakes. Ross Campbell and I talk about this a lot. Anybody can call himself an expert and make recommendations for doing this or that with children. And we get to see the results of such recommendations. I would say, before accepting anybody's advice about childrearing, that you look at what that person does every day. What is his training? Is the person a counselor or not? Anybody can tell you how to raise your children. Until someone has tested the results of his advice, there is no room to suggest ways to help others.

But to get back to your question—any excessive use of guilt, humility, or pressure to be self-effacing can indeed lead to problems. I think balance is the term we used before, and I feel it would work here also.

Question: Don't you think it's impossible to overcome depression without a daily spiritual walk with the Lord?

Answer: A relationship with God is necessary in life. It gives the depth we need to overcome problems. It's a vital part of my life in today's world.

But there is another issue that comes to mind. Many people who get depressed feel that they are being punished for something. I have heard others say, "If you just get right with God, you won't feel depressed."

Now that's unfair. All we have to do is look in the Bible to see that problems arise no matter how close we are to God.

Yes, having a spiritual relationship with God helps me personally overcome my problems. However, I can be depressed and be living close to God at the same time. God does not promise that if we follow Him everything will be marvelous. The disciples' lives and deaths proved that.

Yet, to me, the ultimate depression is being separated from Christ's love. His love is exceptionally powerful. If we can allow ourselves to get out of the way, His love can lift up. In this complex world, however, such simple answers are often overlooked.

Our problems today are serious. But with Christ's love and help we can change.